‖‖‖ ‖‖‖‖‖‖‖‖‖‖‖‖‖‖‖‖‖‖‖‖‖‖‖‖‖

W9-BDZ-913

RICHARD

CHEERS!

TO YOUR CONTINUED

SUCCESS

THE POWER OF CHOICE

A Guide to
Personal and Professional
Self-Management

by
Ted Willey

Berwick House

Copyright © 1988 by Ted Willey

All rights reserved. No part of this book may be reproduced or transmitted in any form or by any means, electronic or mechanical, including photocopying, recording, or by an information storage and retrieval system— except by a reviewer who may quote brief passages in a review to be printed in a magazine or newspaper— without permission in writing from the publisher. For information, please contact The Training Company, Inc./Berwick House, P.O. Box 6198, Denver, CO 80206.

Fourth Printing 1999

Library of Congress Cataloging-in-Publication Data

Willey, Ted
    The power of choice: a guide to personal and professional self-management / by Ted Willey
        p. cm.
    Bibliography: p
    Includes index.
    ISBN 0–929376–92–7: $19.95
    1. Choice (Psychology) 2. Self-realization. 3. Responsibility. 4. Self-management (Psychology) I. Title
BF611.W55 1988
158'. 1—dc 19   88–24087
                                                                          CIP

ATTENTION MANAGERS, ASSOCIATIONS, PARENT ORGANI-ZATIONS, CHURCH GROUPS, GOVERNMENT AGENCIES: Quantity discounts are available on bulk purchases of this book for educational, business, or promotional use. For information, please contact our Special Sales Department at 1-800-637-6106.

To assist you in fully utilizing the information in this book, special training conferences have been developed. These follow up training programs include seminars, videotapes, audiotapes and workbooks. For further information, please contact The Training Company, Inc., P.O. Box 6198, Denver, CO 80206 or call 1-800-637-6106

Printed and bound in the United States of America.

Acknowledgment

A special note of appreciation to Bruce Most for his help, support, and considerable technical expertise. His efforts, patience, and voice of challenge were tremendously valuable. Thanks also to my partner and wife Dorothy, without whose input, organizational ability, and love this book would not have been completed.

Many other individuals including seminar participants, staff, clients, and friends have challenged me intellectually and encouraged the development of this project.

Table of Contents

The main themes and principles of Total Responsibility Management are outlined; each of us is who we choose to be; each of us is totally in control of ourselves; accepting total personal responsibility for ourselves is the key to achieving the choices we want; life is a game like Monopoly.

This chapter focuses on our culture's popular notions of personal responsibility; how we use excuses every day to escape personal responsibility for our actions and our experiences; how we can have happier and more effective personal and professional lives through the principle of 100 percent personal responsibility.

The principle of 100 percent personal responsibility is established; life is a series of nows and we choose each now; how we try to segment responsibility for our experiences; being responsible is different from fault or blame; responsibility is not arbitrary; why we avoid personal responsibility.

How we allow external events and people to control us; how playing from cause is critical to achieving control of our lives; there are no excuses . . . ever!

We are responsible for our feelings; roots of feelings; conditioning as an excuse; inconsistent modeling; the why game;

how we expend more energy making excuses and finding fault with others than we do in getting the job done; packing our own parachute.

A satirical tale about the planet Uranus where things and people really can do it to you.

Examines how most of us live in the past or the future instead of the present, and how living in the present allows us to make better choices.

How and why we allow our bodies to control us; how we choose to be sick; why our body and our spirit are not the same.

Our minds, like our bodies, too often control our choices; living in the future; living in the past; the ladder of the mind; belief systems; the *Unc* fighter.

Lying cheats us of living our lives fully; we are a series of tubes; lies of omission and lies of commission; white lies.

There are no limits except those we choose; "can't" means "won't"; creating new realities; expectations are self-fulfilling; creativity is based in refusing to accept old realities; steel pipe and dot exercises.

A pithy, humorous parable about how each of us is the center of our universe but fail to recognize it.

This chapter explores the concept of how each of us is unique and how that affects our choices; we allow others to define us and we attempt to define others; we learn to seek approval at an early age; we do not need other people; scurvy elephants and artichokes.

This chapter looks at the controversial metaphysical foundation of the principles of total responsibility management, including how we are totally responsible for our own birth and death.

How other people's behavior around us reflects our own behavior; how we can better manage or motivate others by first managing and motivating ourselves; modeling is hard work.

Examples of how ritualistic behavior, from perfunctory greetings to destructive efforts to make others "wrong," limits our personal choices; how we can teach others to learn total responsibility by stopping our rescue of them; the rescue triangle.

Good communication is vital for effective self-management, and the key to good communication is common understanding between people; nuts and bolts discussion of the critical difference between leveling and dumping; how we try to speak for others; effective leveling techniques.

A step-by-step approach, with extended examples, to setting up valuable leveling sessions with bosses, employees, friends, and family.; how to define the rules of the game; making clear duties, goals, responsibilities, authority.

One key to playing life from cause instead of effect is agreements; what happened to the concept of "your word"?; what is an agreement?; how to set up agreements and make them work; altering agreements; how to play from 100% instead of 50–50.

A goal is an agreement with yourself; the difference between a goal and a wish; setting your own goals; exercise for setting short- and long-term goals.

How to get the most out of this book; the ultimate goal of "I" is "We"; some "real world" examples of Total Responsibility Management; The Silver Hammer.

We achieve a destiny which we have chosen.
—Lachalier

Introduction

This is a book about choices: that they are limitless, that they are ours to keep, that we can learn to make more of the choices we want instead of merely suffering the consequences of choices we do not want. This is a book about the most basic choice of all in life:

You are what you choose to be.

For all its complexities, its contradictions and ambiguities, its frustrations and fatalisms, human life really is a simple proposition. You are a product of your own choices. You make decisions every day, every hour, every moment, that determine the state of your life. You choose to be president of the company or you choose to be unemployed, you choose to fall in love or get divorced, you choose to win the lottery, you choose to fall victim to a terminal disease or to become a star athlete. *You* choose . . . no one else chooses for you. No one else does it to you.

You are what you choose to be.

Notice I did not say *want* or *desire* or *wish*. I use the word "choose" to mean selecting or deciding or authoring individual actions that lead to a result. That is, you take the steps . . . you make the decisions . . . you do something or you do not do something that results in your experiencing a consequence, whether it be good or bad.

I can hear you scoffing right now. I know, because I hear the same reaction every time I introduce this principle at my seminars and speeches and in my consulting with businesses across the country. Who, in today's age, believes they have control over their own lives, their own fates? A little control, perhaps, in the best of times, but not *total* control. No, nobody can be totally responsible for all the experiences of their own life in today's complex society.

Don't we as individuals, as a society, as a world blame our experiences on others—especially those experiences we view as undesirable? Don't we find excuses for our inability to function as we want to? Haven't we made ourselves hostages—willing hostages, I would argue—to terrorists, drug dealers, pornographers, child abusers and wife batterers, faulty alarm clocks, Big Business, Big Government, burglars, skin color, Japanese car manufacturers, high interest rates and falling farm prices, chemical imbalances in the brain, bad weather, bad luck, ringing telephones, violent television shows, poor education, genetic heritage, sexist managers, auto mechanics, poverty, corrupt politicians, racists, traffic jams, sugar, horoscopes and biorhythms, drunk drivers, and every other reprehensible being and event we can pin responsibility on?

Haven't we embraced the *angst* of the philosophers, novelists, essayists, historians, and naysayers who speak of humankind's fate as though it belongs in someone or something else's hands, that we are merely corks bobbing in the currents of history or caught up in the sweep of destinies? Haven't we accepted our destinies as programs written by others, as though life were a supercomputer and we were merely the numbers crunched in by an omniscient programmer? Haven't we learned that life is always "doing it to us" instead of the other way around, that external events shape and control and manipulate our experiences? Haven't we learned, often accepted into our very marrow, that life is merely what is "in the cards" or "written on the wall" or the "roll of the dice" or "God's will"? Don't the self-help articles in magazines teach us how to "cope" with the frustrations of life, that we need to merely learn how to "adjust" to those frustrations and exigencies of life that are designed by that vague international conspiracy known as The Others?

Life is a futile gesture against Death, we are taught in a thousand different ways, and the best and easiest thing to do is to grease the skids and enjoy the ride down.

We have become a people who have quit believing in our own destinies. Not a destiny imposed by some order outside ourselves, but a sense of destiny from within, a sense that each of us, and each of us alone, controls our lives. We have lost our sense of purpose and abdicated our selves. We have allowed ourselves to be pawns in the hands of other people and external events. We blame everything we don't like about our lives on others, and in the process diminish ourselves and our personal options.

Yet . . . you are what you choose to be. You are the product of the choices you make in your daily life.

That may sound simplistic, facile, like another instant cultural bromide to scribble on bathroom walls. If people really believed they were something other than victims, if they believed they controlled their own destinies and knew how to manage their own lives, then I could stop right here instead of writing an entire book. Children would grow up in a culture that teaches—and lives—the philosophy that life is the embodiment of limitless choices, that we each are painters with a million colors and hues at our disposal and a blank canvas on which to paint our individual life story.

This is a book about achieving those limitless choices. We will achieve those choices—choices we desire—by exploring and applying to life a new definition of personal responsibility. It is a definition that recognizes that we are *totally* responsible for everything—absolutely everything—that we experience in our lives. This book will not advocate or promote or preach how you should or should not live. That is your choice. Whether you are a brick layer or a politician, whether you have never married or have been married more times than you care to think about, whether you are overweight or drink too much, whether you are an atheist or Jewish or born-again Christian, whether you love or hate the bomb does not matter in this book. What matters is you come to recognize that your life, the experiences you have in your life, the way you see yourself are your choices. Other people and outside "forces" do not choose for you or do it to you.

This is not an easy book. It is a lot easier to go through life blaming everybody and everything else for what happens to you. Anybody can do that. It's easier than falling off a bicycle. This is not an easy book because I do not toss out a dozen short golden rules to live by or ten diet-like prescriptions for changing your lifestyle that you can memorize or take out of your pocket and consult each time you encounter a challenging situation. It is not a book that glibly tells you how to win friends and influence people, how to manage and motivate and control others to do your bidding. It does not tell you how to "fix" the rest of the world or look out for Number One at the expense of others.

No, this is not an easy book. It is a risky book. You will be challenged by new ways to look at life. You will no longer be able to "alibi" your life by pointing your finger at other people or external things or life's "events." Most people go through life looking for a book, a guru, a seminar that will fix things for them. They want someone to overhaul the organization chart for them, so they can manage others at work or their family at home. They want to know how to get their life "organized," how to get others organized, how to make and save more money, how to save "time" as though time was a commodity like wheat. This book offers only one "prescription": consult yourself. Nobody knows what is best for you better than you do. Nobody can manage you better than yourself. As we shall see, *only* you can manage *only* yourself, not others; only you can motivate yourself, not others; only you can control yourself, not others.

Like so many people, I too went searching for answers. What I found I call Total Responsibility Management. It is a self-management style for living, the only management style you will ever need. Total Responsibility Management is an attitude. For individuals to run companies well, I believe they must first run themselves well. For individuals to make relationships work, I think they have to first make themselves work. For parents to be effective, to teach children to be responsible for managing and directing their own lives, I believe those parents must first manage and direct themselves.

As difficult and risky as this may appear at first, once you realize you and only you are in direct control of your being, you and only you can manage your life, then life takes on new and exciting possibilities. Once you recognize that you are completely responsible for what happens to you, then you will be in a position to take charge of your own life. You will recognize that there are more choices and alternatives than you ever thought possible. You will turn failures—and we all fail—into

4

successes. You will feel better about yourself, less inhibited, less frustrated, less the victim and more the doer. Only people who accept responsibility for themselves are able to grow.

The premise that we are totally responsible for all the choices we make in our lives is not new. Indeed, it is a value many of us learned since childhood from our parents, our teachers, our ministers, our politicians, our philosophers. Unfortunately, those values have not been modeled with the same enthusiasm with which they were taught. One only has to look around to realize life is a matter of do what I say, not what I do. Our heroes and our messengers systematically take responsibility when things go well, and bitch and blame and find fault when things do not. Thus, while many of us may intellectually recognize the principles I talk about in this book, we have come to apply them arbitrarily. Often we are not even aware we have other choices, that we do not have to be in the situations we are in.

Most of the principles of total responsibility I describe here are threads already woven through the fabric of our culture, though often they are threads running contradictory to the main pattern of action. My intention in this book is to provide a badly needed review and a deeper insight into the ramifications of these principles than most readers may have thought about. I will explore how we have lost our sense of individual personal responsibility, how we can regain it, how we can apply it effectively so as to function successfully at work and at home: with our kids, our spouses, our friends, our bosses, and our employees.

Some of what I say here will probably shock you or make you angry (actually, you will allow it to shock or anger you). You may likely disagree at points. You may cry and laugh. That's fine. It is not necessary to totally accept everything written here to draw value for yourself. Think of this book as a grocery store, in which you pick and choose what is right for your life.

This is not an esoteric philosophy book, remote from life. It is a participatory book, whose examples and anecdotes are drawn from the working and personal worlds around you, in a way that will have you nodding your heads—what I call *ahas*—in empathy. It is a commonsense book, stressing practical and realistic tools for making us more effective "self-managers."

This book stresses the valuable uniqueness of each of us, that each of us is a limitless reservoir of talent, creativity, knowledge, self-worth, energy, love. But only when we play entirely from cause instead of effect will we be able to fully tap that reservoir.

This is a book about the game called Life. Life is a game, like Parcheesi or Bridge. Earth is a game, the United States of America is a game, Iran is a different game, IBM is a game, farming is a game, marriage is a game. Each game is a serious game, with its own set of rules, and it is necessary to understand those rules when you play that particular game. Often the rules are ill-defined and poorly communicated. The rules of the game called Life are really very clear, yet most of us seem to have forgotten some of them, or refuse to play by them, especially that most basic of rules: You are what you choose to be.

When you were a kid, and perhaps even now, you played a game called Monopoly. Remember? Remember your parents buying the game and bringing it home? The box had a plastic wrapper around it and you tore it off and opened the box and saw for the first time—and the last time—all the little compartments with everything in its place. Among the compartments was a packet of pieces you played with: Scottie Dog, Top Hat, the Shoe, Skate, the Iron, the Thimble. We all picked a piece to play with, and most of us had a favorite piece. Mine was the Thimble. Ever notice that whichever piece we picked was a perfect reflection of our personality or our physical appearance? I never played unless I could be the Thimble.

When you played the game called Monopoly, you grabbed the rule book, and the rule book says the purpose of the game is to go around the board in a clockwise direction, acquire as much property as you can, leverage that property like a Rockefeller, stay away from jail and all the other hazards, hopefully land on Free Parking with something in the middle, shoot for Boardwalk and Park Place, and try to bust your opponents.

Life is a game like Monopoly, and we each play with our piece. My piece is called Ted. Your piece is called Dorothy or Megan or Scott or Ruth or Jeremy or Valerie. And we play on the board called Life and try to stay out of jail and get free parking and win the lottery and raise a healthy family and enjoy our work. This book is a time-out from that game called Life. It is a chance to re-examine how well we are playing the game. What are the rules? Is the game clear? Are we even in the game? Is your life going the way you want it to? Or is it so off the mark, so far from your desires and dreams and hopes that much of the time you merely check out from it? I remember playing life pretty well until I was about 22 and then I checked out until I was 31, and I've been in and out ever since. I want to be in all the time. I want to play this game called Life with my eyes wide open.

If you prefer to live with averageness and mediocrity, if you prefer to make excuses, if you like other people to make decisions for you, if you don't care if people fail to keep their promises to you, if you enjoy lousy service, if you like being unproductive and having those around you unproductive, if you don't mind failing to achieve what you desire in Life, then now is the time to stop reading this book. For those of you, on the other hand, who want to take charge of your life, who want to have more satisfying, more pleasurable choices, then read on. . . .

Responsibility is a unique concept. It can only reside and inhere in a single individual. You may share it with others, but your portion is not diminished. You may delegate it, but it is still with you. You may disclaim it, but you cannot divest yourself of it.

—Admiral Hyman Rickover

1

Hey, It Ain't My Fault

Avoiding personal responsibility has become our nation's most popular pastime. Baseball, football, basketball, and golf combined do not draw the crowds this game does. It is no mere spectator sport, either. When it comes to abdicating personal accountability for one's actions and experiences in one's life, everyone gets into the game. Nobody but nobody takes personal responsibility anymore for anything he or she does—especially if something undesirable is the result. People are willing to take the risks but rarely the consequences. Everywhere you turn people are blaming this or that on someone or something else, save their own ineptness or failure to take charge. In the shirker's world, it is *always* the other guy's fault.

I'm exaggerating, you say? It's only the few? Let's skim the headlines:

- Few of us will ever forget the grim news when it splashed across our television screens in the summer of 1984: a 41-year-old unemployed man named James Huberty walked into a McDonald's restaurant in San Ysidro, California, and gunned down 21 workers and patrons, and wounded 19 more, before SWAT marksmen killed him.

  Two years later Huberty's wife sued McDonald's and another company for $5 million, blaming *them* for her husband's violent rampage. McDonald's, she claimed, contributed to the death of its own patrons and workers because the fast-food chain routinely added monosodium glutamate to their food, which her husband apparently routinely ate. In the same lawsuit she alleged that her late husband's blood had been "poisoned" by high levels of lead and cadmium, which he allegedly was exposed to while working as a welder for a company that makes industrial boilers.

● During the 1986 U. S. Open Tennis Championships in New York, one of the most prestigious tennis events in the world, John McEnroe and his doubles partner, Peter Flemming, were disqualified because they failed to arrive on time for their first-round doubles match. Predictably, both men were upset, McEnroe in particular. "Why couldn't you have waited longer?" demanded the tennis world's *enfant terrible.* "How could you do this?" McEnroe's excuse: They were caught in traffic.

● Probably no one makes more excuses than politicians and government bureaucrats. When the scandal broke publicly in November 1986 over the secret shipments of arms from the United States to Iran in exchange for American hostages, and the diversion of the profits to the *contras* in Nicaragua, President Reagan blamed everyone but his own White House. He especially criticized the bearer of the bad news, saying it would not have been an issue if the press had not exposed it. His personal excuse was, "I was not fully informed."

● I'm not picking on President Reagan. Examine any President and any politician and you will find a consummate excuse-maker. Take former congressman Richard Kelly who excused himself for taking a $25,000 Abscam bribe by claiming he was conducting his own investigation of Arabs.

● People write entire books to blame others. Mary Cunningham was a rising executive at the Bendix Corporation until she fell out of favor following her well-publicized relationship with the chairman of Bendix, William Agee. Cunningham eventually wrote a book, *Powerplay: What Really*

Happened at Bendix, in which she blamed nearly everybody, including the press, for her fall from grace.

- In August of 1986 a part-time postal worker named Patrick Sherrill, faced with dismissal for poor work, walked through a downtown post office in Edmond, Oklahoma, with three pistols and killed 14 supervisors and co-workers, and wounded 6 more before shooting himself to death.

    As if the horror of the killings was not enough, we had to listen to the following excuse by the president of the National Associati n of Letter Carriers:

    "While we are shocked and dismayed by what happened . . . we cannot help but believe that Mr. Sherrill was pushed over the brink by irresponsible and coercive management policies by the Postal Service in the Oklahoma City region." In other words, those dead people asked for it.

- Collective finger-pointing is another way we dilute the principle that each of us is, ultimately, responsible for our own being. If we can get all of society into the act and spread the responsibility around like manure on a field, we can somehow elude the necessity for taking action for ourselves. How many times have you heard or read of people who suffer from poverty, unemployment, racial hatred, and other societal ills say that it is "society's fault." Author James Baldwin spoke for these individuals one evening when on a television show he stared coldly out of the television screen and said, "I've just come from seeing a dead boy—you killed him." The boy turned out to be a 28-year-old man who had died of an overdose of drugs. Apparently it never occurred to Baldwin that the man might have been responsible for his own death.

A Money Maker

Shirking responsibility in this country has become not only a cultural necessity but an economic virtue. I can't think of an easier way, short of winning a state lottery, to make a pile of

11

bucks in this country. What is to be gained by holding yourself responsible for what befalls you in life when you can find some individual or company with a large insurance policy, yell "negligence," and sue the tar out of them. Why bother to earn money the old fashioned way. If Horatio Algier were written today, he'd hire Melvin Belli and file suit against his employer.

Examples:

- In West Virginia, three men suffering from lung cancer sued several tobacco companies to the jingle of $9.3 million. They alleged that the companies had not done enough to warn them of the harmful and "addictive" properties of nicotine.

- A man sued a hotel because he burned himself while taking a shower. Nothing malfunctioned with the hot water system. The guest admits he turned on the shower, stepped into it without testing it, and was scalded. Apparently the hotel was supposed to have a concierge on duty at all times to run the tap water over his wrist like a mother testing her baby's milk.

- A Denver attorney recommended to three of his clients that they pay an out-of-court settlement of $54,000 to avoid trial of a federal lawsuit. The three men ignored his advice, went to trial, and were hit with a $1,062,850 judgment for conspiracy to defraud. What else could they do but pursue their most logical recourse. They sued their attorney for $1.4 million—and won!

- Blaming others for our mistakes and lack of foresight infests our business community as well. Though the evidence is overwhelming that our huge national trade deficit stems primarily from American companies failing to produce quality products at reasonable prices to compete on the open market, American industry and Congress prefer to blame the Japanese and other foreign nations by claiming unfair trade practices.

- Farmers blame high interest rates, low prices, bad weather, and foreign imports for their economic predicament—not the fact that they bought too much expensive farm equipment and put too much unused land into production in the late 1970's.

- Not long ago I read a piece by Mark Patinkin, a writer for the Providence, R. I. *Journal,* who was shocked that a woman who had been one of the hostages hijacked out of Athens on a TWA flight was actually *not* going to sue the airline. Four other passengers had already filed suit. Why not she? the columnist had asked her. "Because everyone has to take some responsibility for their actions," she replied. "Nobody forced us on that plane."

Can you believe that woman? Actually taking responsibility for the consequences of her own actions? Both the columnist and I had the same reaction: it was downright un-American. It has become axiomatic in this nation that if something bad happens to you, blame somebody else and then sue them. If nothing else, at least you'll get your name in the paper along with the thousands of other plaintiffs. As Patinkin pointed out in his column, lawsuits in this country have risen *20 times* faster than the population. There's no better growth industry to invest in.

Closer to Home

Is all this too remote for you? You've never been hijacked or shot at while eating at a fast-food restaurant, John McEnroe always was a punk anyway, and the only time you think about farmers is when you notice vegetable prices going up? Well, you don't have to look far to find all the excuse-making and fault-finding you could possibly want.

- "I would have written sooner, but you know what it's like with three little kids around the house."

- Have you waited an hour past your appointment at the doctor's office because, as the receptionist explains it, the "doctor had an emergency this morning"?

- I just didn't have time.

- Everybody else does it.

- I know it's wrong for him to hit the kids, but he's under a lot of pressure at work.

- I couldn't help it.

- When you lost money on the stock market, was it your stockbroker's fault?

- My watch stopped.

- Sorry I'm late. The meeting ran longer than I expected.

- But mom, it's not my fault. Billy started it.

- It's your fault I'm angry.

- Do you, or parents around you, blame children's unruly behavior, bad eating habits, and mercenary requests for toys on the exploitation and violence of television shows and television advertisers (while continuing to let the children watch those shows)?

- A high school girl's soccer coach recalled in a newspaper article that he spent as much time angrily listening to his players explain why they missed practice or were late as he did coaching them. One of his players assembled a list of 100 of the standard and not-so-standard excuses, and in time the girls would simply call out the number of the excuse when they arrived late for practice. "Number 37!

14

Number 14!" The coach said everyone got a good laugh out of it, though he didn't say if it cut down on the tardiness.

After a while, don't we begin to live our excuses? Ask yourself—in all honesty—when was the last time you heard someone (including yourself) take responsibility for something negative that happened to them? When did you last hear someone say, in effect, "I apologize for being late. I obviously didn't take the responsibility to be here on time."

Deep Trouble

When we start blaming fast-food hamburgers for a person's irrational acts, and accepting that as a plausible excuse, then this country is in deep trouble. Can't you see the TV ads if the killer's widow wins her case against McDonald's:

EAT BUSY BURGERS
THEY NOT ONLY TASTE GREAT . . . THEY DON'T KILL

I think it might warrant an investigation to see if the "coercive" managers who supervised Robert Sherrill, the killer postal clerk in Oklahoma, also ate often at McDonald's. I suspect there's a definite link.

Which is not to say that monosodium glutamate and lead and cadmium are good for our bodies. Certainly we should be careful about what we ingest. But once ingested, can we use that as an excuse for our actions? Should a drunk driver who's killed someone be excused from his or her responsibility (and I'm talking about personal responsibility here, not legal) because the person ingested a liquid that does funny things to the body and the mind? One can argue that once a person becomes drunk, then that person has lost self-control; I argue that the glass of booze didn't care in the first place. It will sit there in that glass until it evaporates and it will not care. The person *chose* to drink, and what happens later is still that person's responsibility.

If blaming monosodium glutamate for one of the most violent

15

mass murders in this nation's history seems as ludicrous to you as it does to me, do you nonetheless accept the more conventional wisdom that a criminal's actions can usually be blamed on a disturbed past such as abuse as a child, poverty, drugs, or emotional stress?

In the case of the McDonald's murderer, criminologists and psychologists were quick to draw their own conclusions about why he slaughtered those people: a deep, suppressed rage; a man with little emotional connections to others; a man from a broken home. That's the common pattern attributed to most random murderers. I'm not going to argue here about the validity or the value of such diagnoses. At best, those conclusions provide useful background as to why some people commit such outrageously violent acts. They are, however, not *excuses* for murder. James Huberty slaughtered 21 people that day in San Ysidro because he *chose* to. (I'll talk later about the people who *chose* to die that day at McDonald's).

When we blame bad air and sugar in our cereal and television advertising for the unacceptable behavior of our children and ourselves, we are in deep trouble.

When our politicians constantly fault the other party, the president, the Japanese, the Russians, and simply "factors beyond our control" for the ills of our nation and the world, we are in deep trouble.

When we blame others for how we feel about ourselves, we are in deep trouble.

When we blame traffic and bad weather for our being late to work, we are in deep trouble.

When we fault genetic inheritance and tobacco for our poor health and our erratic behavior, we are in deep trouble.

Don't get me wrong here. In the case of the men suing the tobacco companies, for example, I am not suggesting that a corporation can be wantonly irresponsible with the products and services it produces. Every company has total responsibility to ensure that its products perform as advertised and neither the products nor the production of those products is harmful to its employees or the public.

16

The company must pay accordingly when it fails to live up to that contract.

With that said, the caution of "Let the buyer beware" still applies to the consumer. Where had those three West Virginia men lived the past 20 years to not have known of the risks of lung cancer from smoking? Why did they not quit smoking once they realized there were risks? Did six-foot-six goons from these tobacco companies physically pin the three down by the arms and blow smoke down their throats until they were addicted? Who, ultimately, suffered the consequences of the smoking? The tobacco companies may end up footing the bill—but who ends up dying from cancer?

Personally, I have no doubt that excessive smoking does harmful things to our bodies, as does the excessive intake of alcohol, lead, monosodium glutamate, and for that matter, water. But I stand by the premise that *tobacco does not cause cancer*. Tobacco does not care. Tobacco is a plant with no brains and no feelings. It will sit out in those fields until it rots and it will not care one iota.

People cause cancer by smoking tobacco.

Flight from Responsibility

In our flight from personal responsibility we as a people are giving up the one trait that most distinguishes us from every other creature on this planet: our ability to choose how to live, our ability to control our own destinies. Increasingly, we are making ourselves "victims" to outside forces. We make drunk drivers victims when we blame the bars for serving them in the first place. When comedian and actor John Belushi died of a drug overdose, some of us thought, "We're sad you died, John, but those are the consequences you suffered for taking that risk." But soon after, a female companion of Belushi's is accused of murder because she helped him administer the fatal dose. Suddenly the message is that perhaps Belushi really wasn't responsible after all for taking drugs.

When our business leaders slough off personal accountability, when they blame everybody and everything else for what ails their company or their industry or the economy at large, then we as individuals suffer through high trade deficits, lost jobs, a sluggish economy, a failure of imagination that is so fundamental to business growth and stability.

We also see the manifestation of this shirking in the direct services we receive. Go to many a hotel in this country and you're likely to find a desk clerk with the airs of a bankrupt duke. Store clerks could care less whether you are served. Auto mechanics are indifferent whether your car is back in two days or two weeks, or whether it is fixed properly. Since everyone figures somebody else is responsible, there is no incentive to put themselves on the line.

When we allow our politicians to hold everybody but themselves responsible for the problems and the solutions in our society, then we have lost effective control of the government we elected. In return, we get an expensive, bloated bureaucracy which we have given permission to program every aspect of our lives—and about which, of course, we blame and complain incessantly.

Most of all, when we make everyone else liable for our behavior and our experiences, we lose the very essences of ourselves. We diminish ourselves each time we blame someone else for what we experience. We have become a society willing to take risks, but not willing to accept the results for those risks. Only when we quit blaming others, only when we realize that each of us, and only each of us, is responsible for our own life will we be able to reach the highest levels of personal achievement, productivity, effectiveness, and happiness.

We make our fortunes and call them fate . . .
—Benjamin Disraeli

2

Packing Your Own Parachute

I've never jumped out of an airplane or parachuted, but it has always looked exhilarating—and more than a little frightening. My understanding of parachuting is you don't just go up and leap out of the plane and release the chute the first time around. You learn the fundamentals before ever leaving the ground. One of those fundamentals is learning how to properly pack your own parachute. Most skydivers pack their own main chutes, and even if they have licensed riggers pack their chute, they still double-check to make certain the chute is in good repair and properly assembled. After all, while people have jumped out of airplanes without parachutes or with failed parachutes and survived, this is not a risk the average person wants voluntarily to take.

Yet . . . most people I know leap out of airplanes every day in their personal and professional lives and never once pack their own parachute or check to see if the damn thing was properly packed by someone else. They *trust* others to have packed the thing (that is, they assume someone else is going to look out for their own best interests), and then when something goes wrong they—or their survivors—sue the packer, the manufacturer of the parachute, the pilot, the plane's mechanic, the guy who pumped gas into the plane, the manufacturer of the airplane, and, if they were still alive, Orville and Wilbur Wright for inventing the airplane in the first place.

I read not long ago that the wife of one of the seven astronauts who died in the fiery Challenger explosion January 28, 1986, is suing the designer and manufacturer of the booster rocket that blew up. I knew as soon as the Challenger exploded (even if it had been blown up by a terrorist's bomb) some of the survivors would sue. After all, bad experiences are always somebody else's fault!

Following the Challenger disaster, public and private investigations ran their predictable courses. Finger-pointing and fault-finding occupied our attention for weeks and months after the disaster. While these criticisms may have been useful for making changes that will prevent future disasters, the doling out of blame and fault-finding and finger-pointing is of absolutely no consolation to the dead astronauts. Indeed, what I found most interesting about the Challenger disaster was that many of those problems were known among the astronauts themselves before the launch.

The questionable safety of the culpable O-rings had been initially raised three years prior to the first shuttle launch. Members of the astronaut corps had raised some of these very concerns. Yet six astronauts and a teacher "innocently" climbed aboard a questionable piece of hardware.

They let somebody else pack their parachutes.

Learning to Pack Our Own

So how do we learn to pack our own parachutes for life? How do we learn to quit blaming everyone and everything else for our own failures to watch out for ourselves? How do we learn to take charge of our life, to become proactive instead of *assuming* others are going to look out for our best interests?

Let's begin with this principle:

Each of us is 100 percent responsible for deciding and causing every experience that occurs within our life.

One hundred percent! Not 80–20 or 50–50 or 30–70! You don't get to parcel out to someone else that portion of your life you don't like. You don't get to say, "I'll take credit for the good things that happen to me, the 70 percent of my life I like, and I'll blame or make responsible the other 30 percent, the part I don't like, the things that go wrong, on others." Let me repeat this principle:

Each of us is 100 percent responsible for deciding and causing every experience that occurs within our life.

Preposterous, you say? How can I have complete control over every aspect of my life? Nobody, not even the very rich and the very powerful, have that kind of control. What about all those other people who are doing things to me? They're the ones responsible for the fact my car wasn't fixed on time or I missed going to the movie because my daughter was ill or I didn't get my report into my boss on time because my co-author didn't finish his portion when he was scheduled to. They're the ones responsible for my failures, not me.

Reprinted by permission: Tribune Media Services

The word "responsibility" is used many different ways by people. The most common associations we have are that responsibility means the assigning of blame or accountability in a legal sense; finding fault with someone or something; a duty or obligation to do something. I use the word "responsibility" here and throughout the book as "that which is attributed to being the cause" of something. Being responsible means *causing* something to happen.

How do we know what the causes are for our experiences? How can we take personal responsibility for everything that happens to us?

Because results do not lie.

Life is a composition of moments, a string of uninterrupted "nows" from the moment we are born to the moment we die—

your latest nows are as you read these words. There is no such thing as time, only "nows." The past was once a now. The moment you woke up this morning was, at that instant, a now. Twenty years ago? . . . A now. Tomorrow morning will be another now. When the future arrives the then will be a now. Notice that nothing ever happens in any other moment other than right "now." Nothing happens in the future until the future becomes a now; nothing happened in the past except that moment when it was a now.

If I look back over my life, the results of my nows will show me that nothing has ever happened any other way than the way it did. Every now on earth never happened any other way than the way it did. The nows may not be what we wanted or wished them to be, but they were exactly the way they happened. The future nows may not necessarily be what we wish or desire, but they certainly will be what we choose or cause or decide ourselves to experience in those moments of now.

If results lied, if our experiences lied, then they would be something other than the way they were. If we were able to run our life backwards, we would always be able to make all "right" decisions; we would be able to alter our past nows. If life could be run forward, like the film on a VCR, then we could see our future nows and decide whether we want to play them or not. But the fact is, Hollywood time travel aside, life is one surprise party after another.

The main difficulty most of us have in accepting the principle of total personal responsibility is in understanding what in reality is the cause of the results of our nows. Look at it another way. Do you not always suffer the consequences of *your* "nows," of the experiences in your life—good and bad experiences—regardless of who else is to "blame"? No one else can experience your experiences for you.

We have been taught or have learned the perception that we are not responsible for many of our actions and the consequences of those actions. We have accepted the perception that some things are simply beyond our control. We hold other people or other things such as "bad luck" or the "weather" responsible for those consequences. We may accept responsibility for things we understand, but never for things we do not understand or do not know about. Yet each of us, and only each of us alone, can uniquely feel the impact or the consequences of those nows, whether we understand them or not. Whether or not you believe you are responsible for the choices you make, who is the only person to end up sucking pond water with a straw?

Experiencing the Consequences

In October of 1984 a Denver jury awarded a Texas man and his wife $9.4 million in damages from Budget Rent-A-Car for paralytic injuries she sustained in a head-on collision in snowy conditions on a Colorado mountain pass. According to court testimony, the couple and their two children from Corpus Christi, Texas, had specifically requested that snow tires be put on their rental car at Stapleton International Airport in Denver before they set off for a Christmas skiing holiday at a Colorado ski resort. During the trial, experts testified that the two rear tires were "severely worn" street tires instead of adequate snow tires, and hence the reason the car went into a skid on the snowy mountain pass. As to why the driver had not been alarmed by the condition of the tires, he said, " . . . being from down here (Texas), I didn't know anything about them."

Who is responsible for the accident? Who "caused" the accident to occur?

I am not talking about legal responsibility here. That is a question of who is at fault and who is to blame legally. Whether Budget Rent-A-Car is legally responsible or not (the case is under appeal) has no bearing on the results of the "now" of the accident. The legal procedures are conducted only to determine who is going to pay the hospital bills—with "revenge" money thrown in. Personal responsibility and legal fault and blame often have little in common. Legal responsibility is a matter of dispensing "justice," and as anyone knows, justice is at best a tenuous matter in the world, usually determined and administered by one or more people other than the individual who experienced the results.

But who "caused" the now of the accident? Who is personally responsible for the family experiencing that devastating crash?

Let's trace it from the beginning. Who decided that the Texas family should come to Colorado to ski in the first place? . . . Budget Rent-A-Car? Who chose that particular time to come? Who flew into Stapleton Airport? Who chose Budget to provide them with a rental car? Any problem so far accepting the fact the Texas family made those decisions, those choices? That's pretty clear cut, right?

Now we all know that if you come to Colorado during the winter time to ski you are apt to experience snow on the highways. The family from Texas recognized this and specifically requested, wisely, that snow tires be placed on their car. Up to now I think we can all agree that the family made certain decisions or choices, that they were in fact *totally responsible* for taking a series of actions that resulted in their arrival at Stapleton Airport and the Budget Rent-A-Car lot.

It is at this point, their arrival at the Budget lot, that the family appeared to quit taking responsibility for their actions. For instance, any experienced driver, regardless of what state he or she is from, should recognize "severely worn" street tires when they see them. (Being an inexperienced driver, by the way, does not alleviate one from the responsibilities of driving; run down a small child in the street and see if you can use inexperience as an excuse.) And if he did not know what snow tires looked like, did it not behoove him to find out, especially since he had made a special request for them? Did this man even glance at the tires before leaving the lot? Did his wife? If they knew nothing about snow tires, and since it was obvious that the tires were worn, why didn't they go to the rental agency personnel and ask for someone familiar with snow tires to check the tires to see if they were what the man had requested? If the agency refused, or the person who checked the tires appeared perfunctory in his or her inspection, the man and his wife could have taken their business elsewhere. The last I checked there was more than one business willing to rent automobiles, especially in a large airport like Stapleton.

Again, whether or not Budget Rent-A-Car displayed callous

neglect in the renting of the automobile to the family is a legal question. Regardless of the settlement of the issue, the family cannot "blame" Budget for the accident. They remained totally responsible at all times for all of their nows they experienced, including the accident and the paralysis of the mother. Had the trip been successful, would the couple have attributed that success to Budget Rent-A-Car, or anyone else?

Why did they leave the nows of their family—nows they were clearly aware of—in the hands of someone else?

If the legal system could in some way restore the woman's health, could in some way turn back the clock far enough for the family to avoid the accident in the first place, then the need for personal responsibility would not matter. But the clock cannot be turned back. The woman is permanently crippled. She and her family experienced the consequences of their own actions (a lack of action is always a form of choice, by the way), their own irresponsibility. Whether Budget ever pays a penny or not will never change that fact.

Each person is 100 percent responsible for every now that occurs within that person's life.

Results do not lie.

And I believe that if more of us took more responsibility for causing our nows we would have more nows that would be satisfying or pleasurable.

Segmenting Responsibility

As we observed in Chapter One, this same attitude of buck passing, of allowing someone else to watch out for our best interests and then blaming them when something negative happens to us, plagues our professional work lives as well as our personal lives. Employees blame their managers, their managers blame the employees and the unions, and everyone joins together to blame OPEC, the Japanese, taxes, foreign steel manufacturers, Korean clothing sweat shops, Taiwanese product counterfeiting rings, and the communists. What responsibility is taken is segmented; people hold themselves responsible for only a percentage of the effectiveness of the organization. This is a way to hedge their bets.

If I walk into my local utility company with a problem on my electric bill I do not want to hear someone say, "That's not my area of responsibility, sir." I expect them to say, "Yes, sir, let me see what I can do for you. I'll take you to someone over here and tell them what your problem is." If you do not think you are 100 percent responsible for the effectiveness of that public utility or government organization you work for, go to a party some evening and tell people where you work . . .

Unfortunately, most employees in companies bring to work, like a bologna sandwich in their brown bags, the belief that they are only responsible for a percentage of a given operation. They see responsibility divvied up 5 percent . . . 30 percent . . . 20 percent . . . 45 percent. This attitude of "it is not my job, that is not my responsibility," is reinforced by most corporate management personnel and corporate cultures. So like a hand with the fingers separated, employees work independently of each other, and sometimes in conflict of each other. Yet each is, in fact, *100 percent responsible,* and if a company can convey that principle to its employees it will make those fingers come together, unifying into a tight and effective fist.

Let's examine the headlines again. We've all read accounts of businesses, small companies and entire corporations going belly up. For the sake of an example, let's pick an airline that has gone under, throwing out into the streets thousands of pilots, flight attendants, luggage handlers, ticket agents, mechanics, and executives. Some of you may have experienced that horrible feeling of suddenly having to worry about how you're going to pay the mortgage and put food on the table, the humiliation and anger of losing your job, the sadness at losing contact with people with whom you've worked. And if you've never lost your job, you undoubtedly know friends or family members who have.

For a moment, put yourself in the position of a pink-slipped airline employee. What do you tell your family? Who do you blame? Who caused the failure of the airline, which may have had a reputation for on-time service, a nearly flawless safety record, and for pampering its customers? Who is responsible for the loss of your job?

Naturally there are plenty of people at whom to point your finger. You could blame the government for deregulating the airline industry, OPEC for the high cost of jet fuel, predatory competitors, a recalcitrant union, and of course, the executives and the president of the airline for their failure to manage the company properly. The buck always stops at the desk of the company president, right?

I'm sure if you polled your fellow former employees you would find that they blamed or held responsible somebody else for their experiencing their own loss of employment. Nobody says he or she is *personally* responsible for being laid off. But ask yourself this. Did anyone else choose for you to work for that company when you hired on five years ago? Did you not take personal credit—that is, responsibility—for causing yourself to accept the job, and to continue to work there until the day the airline shut down? Did anyone else besides you experience the loss of *your* job?

Far more people than the employees at the airline also experienced the pain of the shutdown. There is your immediate family, of course. There is also the food service which provided the in-flight meals, the airline's outside public relations firm, dozens of other creditors now faced with losing some or all of the money the airline owed them at the time, and of course the thousands of passengers who found themselves inconvenienced when the airline quit flying. (How many of those passengers, would you guess, knew the airline was in trouble but chose to fly the airline anyway?) The ripples from such events always spread wide—as does the blame.

Conventional wisdom would dictate to most of us the notion that none of the above individuals chose to experience the failure of the airline, though we all would assign responsibility (read "blame") for the failure to specific individuals or groups of individuals such as the the executives of the airline. I say conventional wisdom is wrong.

The fact is, every person who in any way was directly or

indirectly affected by the collapse of the airline was *100 percent responsible for experiencing the failure of that airline.*

This is not to say fault or blame for its collapse, or that you were responsible for the responsibilities of other individuals within the airline or the union or the government. You are not responsible for the decisions and actions taken by others, but you are responsible for experiencing the *consequences* of those decisions and actions. This may seem like mere semantics upon first reading, but read again what I just said. As an (imaginary) employee of the airline, you are responsible for experiencing the results of those decisions and actions.

Isn't that all that really counts in life—the results that you personally experience? You and only you, *caused* you to be in your position with the airline. You took the steps—hiring on, reserving a flight, contracting out your services—that lead to your experiencing the airline going belly up. We all do what we know how to do when we do it. If it works, great. If it doesn't, we say I didn't know that was going to happen.

But personal responsibility, whether in your professional or in your personal life, is not something you can arbitrarily turn on and off whenever you wish. You either believe and accept you are responsible for everything that happens to you in your life, or you believe you are responsible for nothing. There is no middle ground, no shirking of responsibility when it suits your own ends. If you are going to play a game, don't you have to play by consistent rules if you are to play at all?

Responsibility Is Not Arbitrary

It has been my experience that the only thing that truly counts in this world is individual responsibility. Love, achievement, happiness, growth, and all the other vital aspects of human development derive from the accomplishments of individual actions, from self-management, from the positive attitude with which we play the game called Life. I contend that if more people recognized this fact, fewer would experience automobile accidents or cancer or unemployment or crime. There are no *victims* in this world. Each person's experiences rest entirely in his or her own hands. The buck does not stop at the president's desk . . . it stops at everybody's desk.

On Friday, at 10 a.m., you had a report due on your boss's desk. As a manager, you delegated portions of that report to two of your employees. One of them failed to complete their assigned work, and consequently your report was not finished by the time prescribed. Can you make the excuse to your boss that the employee under you *caused* you to fail to turn in the report on time?

Before you answer, ask yourself one question: Is my boss going to care who *I* blame? Who made the agreement in the first place? Whose butt is going to get chewed out for failing to deliver the report? It is your report not sitting there on the boss's desk. As a manager, you have the authority to delegate the work of that report to others. But the delegation of that work does not also sanction the delegation of your total responsibility for ensuring that the work is properly completed by the time prescribed. You are still 100 percent responsible——not 50 percent! Would you accept the same excuse if you sat behind your boss's desk?

As hard as many of us struggle to shift the responsibility for our misfortunes onto the shoulders of others, it is a futile effort, for in reality we can never truly relinquish or lose personal responsibility to someone or something else. We may think we do. We may act as if we have, as did the family from Texas who "trusted" Budget Rent-A-Car to watch out for them. We may disclaim our personal responsibility but we cannot divest ourselves of it, as Admiral Rickover so painfully experienced when he was accused of accepting gifts from General Dynamics in return for his influence in their receiving government contracts. Because we are the creators of our own Life Experiences, such divestment is impossible. You cannot deed your personal responsibility—your experiences—over to someone else as if it were a chunk of real estate. You cannot sell it, barter it away, subcontract it, parcel it out, subtract from it, or ignore it . . . at least not at your own peril.

Despite our verbal and intellectual abandonment of personal

responsibility, despite the weary feeling that we have lost control of our lives, despite our willingness—no, our eagerness—to hand our fates over to others, we cannot shed ourselves of the fact that each of us remains 100 percent responsible for the experiences in our life. You are the only person who has absolute control over yourself.

What we have lost is our *sense* of personal responsibility, of control. We have come to *believe* others are in control of what happens to us, which is why we find fault with others when something occurs we do not like. The tragedy of this is that when we blame others, when we try to divest ourselves of our responsibility, the only thing we succeed in doing is reducing the conscious choices we have in our lives. We forfeit the ability to direct our choices toward the goals we wish or desire. The act of not choosing is still choosing because we experience the consequences either way. We cannot avoid making choices for each of our nows. What we can do is make fewer undesirable choices.

If you had recognized that you have total responsibility for your Life Experiences, you would not have allowed that employee to fail to complete on time his or her contribution to your report. You would have communicated to the person the urgency of delivering a well-done report to you on time. You would have been proactive and creative in preventing the late situation from occurring.

Why We Avoid Responsibility

One reason I think many people today balk at the idea of accepting total responsibility for their own experiences is they equate responsibility with guilt and blame and fear of failure. If we admit responsibility for our misfortunes or behavior, we often see that as condemning ourselves. Self-condemnation means feeling guilty, feeling pain. You may have been taught at Our Lady of Perpetual Sorrow and Guilt Forever that experiencing guilt is the only avenue to personal growth. But being 100 percent responsible for your actions has nothing to do with guilt or innocence. Feeling guilty about something you did, or blaming someone else so you will not feel guilty about what happened to you, merely stifles your ability to learn from your experiences.

The great value of recognizing and accepting total responsibility for ourselves is that by not denying our experiences, good and bad, we can apply what we learn to the next now, so it will more likely be a pleasant experience. If we attempt to pass off our responsibility to someone else, then nothing is learned.

Another reason we balk lies in the legal connotations of the word "responsible." In the legal sense, someone who is found "responsible" for some action usually ends up paying a fine or a civil judgment, or goes to jail. The game of legal and not legal in our adversarial court system means right and wrong. If you are responsible for something, you must be "wrong." Since nobody wants to be wrong, we often make excuses and try to blame others. Acknowledging 100 percent responsibility for our behavior and our actions, on the other hand, is a positive approach. It puts down no one. It blames no one. It makes no one wrong. You're not at fault for coming to work late, but you are responsible for it; that is, you "caused" yourself to be late. Once acknowledged who is in control, it is easier to change the habits that make you late in the first place.

Shirking personal responsibility is also a form of laziness. If we can get by in life blaming others, it means we don't have to make decisions and take risks and *do* something. By accepting irresponsibility as the norm, by accepting others' excuses such as the traffic or the weather or "the other guy did it to me," we make it easier on ourselves whenever we fail to take responsibility. On the other hand, if we say, "I won't accept lateness as an excuse," that means we sure as hell better not be late ourselves.

Accepting the principle of 100 percent responsibility for your experiences is not a harsh, burdensome, guilt-ridden philosophy to live by. Accepting total personal responsibility for yourself means recognizing that you can make life better for yourself, that you have far more choices than you ever realized, that choices can make a difference, that you and only you are the author of your own actions, the controller of your own nows, the chooser of your own choices.

Personally, I cannot envision a more joyous, liberating attitude by which to live your life.

We have forty million reasons for failure, but not a single excuse.
—Rudyard Kipling

3

Why Do You Do That to You, Charlie Brown?

One of my cherished fall rituals, and I suspect one of yours, is reading the annual Peanuts comic strip where Charlie Brown attempts to kick a football held by Lucy. Each year Lucy tells Charlie Brown that she will hold the football so he can kick it. Each year Charlie Brown wavers, remembering that last year and every year before that Lucy always yanked the ball away at the last moment so he fell on his butt. Each year Lucy acts sincere and offers some plausible-sounding argument for why *this* year will be different. Each year Charlie Brown inevitably bites, races determinedly across the yard, and falls flat on his butt when Lucy yanks the football away at the last moment.

Doubtless many of you, after reading that strip, feel sorry for Charlie Brown and angry at Lucy. Certainly Lucy is not being very nice. But isn't there a part of you that says to yourself, if only subconsciously, "Charlie Brown, you stupid kid! Why do you do that to you?"

After all, Lucy has been tricking Charlie Brown forever. When is Charlie Brown going to learn? Does he not always *assume,* if only after much demurring, that Lucy will not snatch it away at the last moment? When he does end up on his butt, does he not always blame her, not himself, for doing it to him? What Charlie Brown does not get through his thick round head is that he is choosing to be done to. Who is causing him to have that problem? Lucy is not doing it to him. He is allowing himself to be done to by Lucy. Lucy cannot yank the ball away from Charlie Brown at the last moment unless Charlie Brown agrees in the first place to try to kick the ball.

copyright 1986 United Features Syndicate, Inc.

We All Are Charlie Browns

I think all of us, to one degree or another, are Charlie Browns. (All of us are Lucys, too, but that is another book.) We allow ourselves to be done to. We set ourselves up as victims. No, you protest? You do not see yourself as Charlie Brown? Ever? Only occasionally? More often than you care to admit to yourself?

Do you agree that at least some of the time you feel controlled by other people or "forces" that are external to you? That is, you believe that things happen to you or affect you—caused by other people or external events—that are beyond *your* control? I'm sure you remember the car that smashed into your car at the intersection when you had the green light. Or the stock you bought three days before Black October. Or when your son came down with chicken pox the day before the family was scheduled to leave for a week-long trip to Disneyland.

34

Those experiences were the fault of external forces, right? The other driver . . . A stupid stockbroker . . . A virus . . . Beyond your control . . . Bad luck.

We do not take responsibility for ourselves because our biorhythms are at a critical juncture or our moon is over our cusp and up our valley. We do not take responsibility because of a thyroid condition or our birth order ("I was the last child, you know") or because our parents didn't like us because we were a surprise. The reason we have difficulty developing meaningful relationships today is because we weren't hugged enough when we were babies or because our father was an alcoholic or because we're a Virgo.

I went through a divorce once. You know what *she* did to me? Do you *know*? She caused the divorce. She wouldn't listen to me. She was self-centered. She didn't understand. She wasn't growing at the same pace I was. She wanted all my time.

I want to start my own company, but I can't. Why? Because of my kids, of course. I have to pay for their schooling and their food and their clothes, so I can't afford to quit my job. I'm going to have to wait until my retirement before I can do what I really want to.

For these people, no matter what they do in life it is "out of my hands" or "that is just the way it is and there is nothing I can do about it" or "you can't fight city hall." I call this attitude playing from *effect*.

Charlie Brown is the archetype of the victim. He plays the game called Life from effect, not cause. He *allows* the external world—events and other people—to do things to him instead of him taking charge of himself, instead of being responsible for his own actions.

Perhaps as a child you were taught that you always suffer the consequences of your own actions. You believe that sincerely and deeply. You know it to be true. But do you act that way *100 percent of the time*? Do you not sometimes act like Charlie Brown?

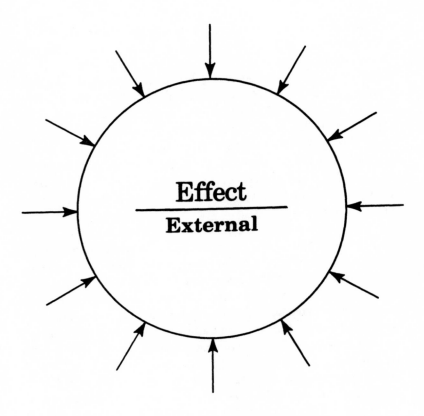

Weathering Our Behavior

The influence of the weather on us is one of the most common and pervasive examples of playing from effect. The weather dictates not only what we will wear for the day, but how we will feel and act.

What a beautiful day . . . Have you heard what the weather is supposed to be like today? . . . Can you believe this weather? What a bummer . . . What's the weather like at your end of the country? . . . I hope the weather is good tomorrow. We want to go on a picnic . . . I hate rainy days.

No wonder weather forecasters have become society's electronic priests.

We even suffer weather-related diseases. Most of us at one time or another have contracted "spring fever" or, snowbound in Buffalo, came down with "cabin fever." Even history's great minds have reacted like puppets on a string when it comes to atmospheric conditions. Voltaire wrote that he was "susceptible to the east wind," Goethe described himself as a "living barometer," and Lincoln was often moody during cold snaps. And all of us have on occasion been "under the weather." Suicide rates climb during rainy weather, and killers in southern California blame their mad acts on the fierce Santa Ana winds.

On Christmas Day in 1982, Denver citizens chose to experience the worst snow storm in the city's history—24 inches in 24 hours. I was smart enough to have left Christmas Eve with my family to fly to Lake Tahoe. I was dumb enough to come back four days later. My family and I came through the airport terminal and ran smack into a wall of bodies and baggage. Outside, transportation anywhere was nearly nonexistent. One taxi was left, 30 people stood impatiently in line for it, and two of them were in a fistfight.

Does weather affect our attitudes and our actions?

A System of Equations

It's Monday. We all know what Mondays are like. We even assign colors to Monday. Blue or gray. And when you look out the window of your bedroom you feel even more blue-sad. The sky is ash gray, like the file cabinet in your office. The whole sky, in fact, looks like a giant file cabinet, which reminds you of the week of work in front of you. The file cabinet in the sky pulls out its "rain" file and dumps on you. The rain *causes* several accidents and traffic creeps along. You are half an hour late to work. When you get to work you have a performance report to finish for tomorrow, but now the rain has put you in such a foul mood you know you are not going to finish the report on time. Then an employee comes into your office to tell you one of the computers has just broken down, and in response you chew out the employee.

37

This string of events is what I call a system of equations.

A = Monday
B = Rain
C = Traffic jam
D = Performance report
E = Computer failure
A + B + C + D + E = *Bad Day*

Now it is Friday. What equation do we usually associate with Fridays?

A = Friday
B = Sunshine
C = Payday
D = Three-day weekend
A + B + C + D = *Good day, baby!*

For many of us the length of the equations grows longer with age. My grandmother ran from A to Q. Everybody knows somebody in life like my grandmother. Nothing is ever right. The sun is shining but she'd say, "I've got to pull the weeds." Ask her if her back is feeling better and she would reply, "Yes, but now my feet hurt." Heaven help her if she felt too cocky or too confident. The weather was always too hot or too cold or we hadn't had enough rain and the grass was dead or we had had too much rain and now she had to mow the grass.

You know the type. They walk around frowning a lot. Like Li'l Abner's character, Joe Btfsplk, a black rain cloud hangs over them constantly. Why did God do this to me? Their entire attitude and expectations spell doom and gloom, and people hate to be around them. They play life totally from effect. Their view of life is simple:

Life is a flat bitch . . .

. . . and then you get to die.

One meets a lot of Joe Btfsplks at work. They make everything and everyone external to them responsible for the condition they are in, for their failure to carry out their assigned tasks, for their inefficiency and ineffectiveness, for their lack of creativity. I've worked for some large corporations, and I listened to these people's excuses every day. I used to make those excuses myself. I bet you know by heart the same lines I heard.

> I've tried to talk to my boss but it doesn't do any good.
> I'd get more work done if I didn't have so many interruptions.
> That is not my area of responsibility.
> You just can't find good people to work for you any more.
> The copy machine broke down.
> The meeting took longer than I anticipated.
> I wish I could make my people more responsible.
> I work my tail off and no one appreciates me.

Ever notice that these same people never have any trouble taking credit for the *positive* things that happen to them. For instance, they never have any problem claiming personal responsibility for getting to work on time. They set their alarm, get up, shower, dress, eat, start the car, drive through traffic, park, and get to their desks by their appointed time. They do this most days of the week. Do you ever hear them say? "Boy, am I glad everybody else was responsible for my getting here on time today. I couldn't have made it without my alarm clock working properly, without my husband fixing my breakfast on time, and without all those nice drivers out there avoiding accidents and moving along smartly so I could make it here today."

But watch that person come in late and what do you hear? "Damn alarm clock stopped in the middle of the night on me. They don't make 'em like they used to. And the traffic! My god, I've never seen so many lunatics on the road. The accidents. The radio said there were twelve this morning and I think I got behind every one of them. One had fifteen cars piled up. Fifteen cars! *Nothing* was moving."

"I'm not interested in excuses, Mildew. You're four minutes late."

HERMAN COPYRIGHT 1986 UNIVERSAL PRESS SYNDICATE. Reprinted with permission. All rights reserved

Another favorite excuse of mine is telephones. How many people do you know at work—or for that matter, how about yourself—who blame their telephone for their inability to complete a report or get the work done they are responsible for? You know the excuses: That phone of mine rings a hundred times a day . . . How's a person supposed to get any work done around here with the phone interrupting me every five minutes . . . It's a miracle I get anything done. What these people fail to realize is that it is *they*, not the telephone, who are causing themselves to have the problem.

Go ahead and make your telephone responsible for your problems. Notice that your telephone *does not care!*

The last time I looked, a telephone was a mere collection of inanimate wires and computer chips and resistors. It can ring all day long and it will not care if you do not answer it. You will not hurt its feelings if you ignore it or if you transfer your calls to the front desk or route them into an answering machine or if you make clear to everyone you do business with that you will accept calls only during certain hours. Trust me. That phone does not care. It will not leap off your desk and clamp its receiver to your ear nor attempt to strangle you with its cord like some technological horror movie. Nor will it cry or make you feel guilty by whining about how lonely it is. Once you understand you are in control, not the telephone, then management of your phone calls becomes a simple matter of you deciding what is best for you.

If each of us is 100 percent responsible for *every* experience that occurs within our lives, then it is impossible for us to be controlled by external events or by other people. The issue is not time or stress or health management. It is Self-management.

No Excuses . . . Ever!

One of my own rules of self-management is to be on time to my seminars and speeches and appointments. There are no excuses . . . ever! Several years ago I contracted to do a program for a hotel company in Milwaukee. It had been an exceptionally bad winter for the Midwest and I was concerned I would not be able to fly in directly. I took the precaution of looking into booking a charter flight, and did book a rental car, as well as a train from Denver to Oakland to Minneapolis. As it turned out, I was able to fly into Milwaukee. But there was no way I could not be there. The president of the hotel company told me he knew I would be there, that he expected me to parachute in if necessary. How many seminars or lectures or music concerts have you gone to at which the speaker or the performer was late, or worse, failed to show?

Learning to play from an attitude of cause instead of effect is difficult. One fall, I and the participants in one of my management seminars chose to experience an unusually heavy mid-October snowfall the second day of the seminar in Denver. Even if you do not live in Colorado, you may remember that snowstorm. It struck during the middle of a Denver Bronco-Green Bay Packer football game being broadcast on national television. By morning, the snow was deep enough that cars were drifted in and the area police departments warned motorists to stay off the roads unless travel was absolutely necessary. Several participants in my seminar were late and six never made it at all.

Why did some people make it and others not, when all experienced the same snowfall? Why did some keep their commitment while others failed? The ones who did not make it made the snow responsible for their failure, naturally. They did not realize, or accept the fact, that snow does not do it to you. Snow does not care.

The people who attended the seminar chose to live in Colorado or chose to come to Colorado to attend the seminar. Everyone knows it snows in Colorado during the winter, and sometimes early in the fall. Thus, one should have no excuse for being unprepared for snow. Those who did not make it could have left earlier for the seminar that day or borrowed a friend's four-wheel drive vehicle or taken one of several other options to ensure that they made it to the seminar on time.

Did Ted Willey make it to the seminar? . . . Did I dare not to? It was my professional responsibility to be at work on time. Would it have been okay to the participants who did make it if I had not? I had made a commitment, just as they had. How can you expect people to believe in, and thus act upon, what you say and what you want if you do not follow it yourself—*100 percent of the time?* As did every participant in the seminar, I knew twelve hours before the second day of the seminar that it was snowing. At one o'clock that morning, not long after the Bronco-Packer game finished (the football players and many fans did not let the snow deter them), I drove to my office, located in the same building as the seminar meeting room, and slept on the couch. Any of the seminar participants would have been welcome to sleep in my office if they too had come down that early.

If you do not mind your employees or your friends choosing to be late whenever it snows or rains because they have seen you choose to come late, fine. You get what you put out. I have no problem with someone choosing not to come. Old habits, old ways of thinking are difficult to change quickly. What is important to me is that people recognize that they cannot blame their lateness on the weather. It is their choice to be late. By acknowledging their responsibility, by acknowledging that they blew it, they will be more anticipatory and proactive and take more responsibility the next time the first snowflake falls.

Most of the seminar participants went to bed that Monday night after it had already snowed for several hours. They had watched it snow heavily during the football game. Yet they went to sleep, got up at their usual time in the morning, looked out their window, and yelled, "Holy cow! Look at all that snow!"

Stop making other people and outside forces responsible for doing it to you! Once you recognize that you are the creator of your own experiences, that you choose what happens to you, that you can play from cause and not effect, then you will not allow anything so minor as bad weather to prevent you from keeping a commitment.

I have a sign in my office that says, No Excuses Accepted . . . Ever! Can you envision a world in which everyone lived by that? In which your children and your boss and your congressional representatives and the store clerks and lawyers and union leaders and everyone else produced results, not excuses? Took responsibility for their own actions, not evasive tactics? Can you imagine how well your company or your marriage or your relationships with your children would function if everyone involved played from cause instead of effect?

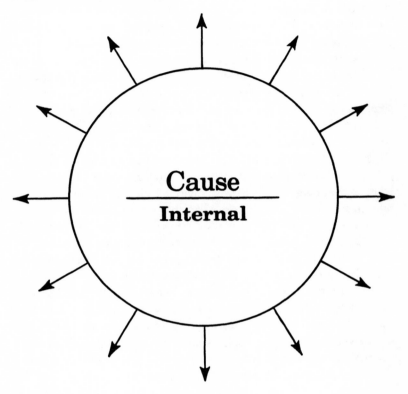

"I'd like to acknowledge my responsibility for not being here on time. I'm aware of that. It will not happen again."

It may happen again. Mistakes and problems occur in the best of worlds. Habits are difficult to change. (Remember, you cannot use that acknowledgment as an excuse.) But you can be certain the mistakes will not occur as often as they did before. Not if total personal responsibility is part and parcel of your life.

44

To know and not to do is still not to know.
—A Chinese proverb

4

Due to Circumstances Beyond....

Snowstorms and telephones are relatively easy examples of how people play from effect instead of cause. While at one time or another we all hold telephones or the weather responsible for our experiences, I think most of us recognize, when we think about it, that neither the weather nor telephones really care. We allow them to affect us. But what about other people? Do people "cause" us to experience what we feel and do? Do other people make us angry? Sad? Happy? (How does the song go?—"You make me happy/When skies are gray"). Do they do it to us?

I went to the grocery store one day, loaded up my grocery cart, and discovered as I stood in the checkout line about ready to pay that the only thing in my checkbook was deposit slips. This is a joint checkbook. My wife, Dorothy, had used the last check and failed to put in a new packet of checks. I'm standing there like an idiot in the line, the clerk smiling her grocery-store smile at me and the people behind me in line waiting impatiently, and I launch into this tirade about how it was my wife's fault for failing to put new checks in the book and that I just didn't know what was the matter with that woman.

Was my wife responsible for me standing there in line without checks, for launching into the tirade, for feeling like a fool? She was 100 percent responsible for failing to put new checks in the book, and she was 100 percent responsible for the experience of having to listen to me complain to her when I got home. But I was also 100 percent responsible for my experience at the store. Was I the one who had gone to the store? Had I checked the checkbook before I left? Was I the one who chose to get angry at the store?

Results do not lie.

Why did I do that to me, Ted Willey?

Authoring Your Feelings

If we are 100 percent responsible for every experience that occurs within our lives, then it is impossible for us to be controlled by external events or by other people.

You're at the dinner table. You're tired after a long day at work, or a long day at the grocery story, K-Mart, dance lessons, soccer practice, play group, and a trip to the library. The last thing you need is to argue with the children. Dinner is the family's quiet time together, a time without television, a time to enjoy food and talk about the day. It is, of course, anything but! Your daughter is showing her brother, who sits across from her, what the inside of her mouth looks like stuffed with mashed potatoes. He laughs, and the Jello in his mouth falls out onto his creamed corn, which causes him and his sister to laugh hysterically. She laughs so hard she knocks her full glass of milk over and it spreads across the table like a small flash flood, eventually cascading over the edge into your lap.

You bolt from your chair, simultaneously slamming your fist down on the table (chipping your dinner plate in the process) and lashing out at your daughter.

"Look at this mess! Look what you made me do! If you'd quit horsing around at dinner none of this would happen. Who taught you your table manners, Genghis Khan? I haven't had an enjoyable meal with you at this table in weeks. You make me so mad! Go up to your room, and I don't want to see your face until tomorrow morning."

Sound familiar? Any *ahas* with that one? Notice you have just made your daughter responsible for not only the situation, but for your feelings and your actions. *You make me so mad.* She provoked you to lose your temper. She *caused you* to break your own plate. She is disrupting everyone at dinner. She is to blame—for everything.

But is she? Was it really your daughter who "made" you mad? You had no choice in the matter? She physically forced your fist to slam onto the plate through some sort of telekinetic power? Or did you choose—all by yourself—to become angry?

Roots of Anger

This last question invariably sparks a variety of responses from people. Many feel that anger is a matter of long-term environmental conditioning, something we have absolutely no control over. One person who felt this way told me she was glad she felt anger at times. The last time she had felt angry had been at an unruly patron in a bar she was managing. The anger enabled her to throw the patron out.

Many students of anger would agree with her. Some social scientists view humans as victims of permanent aggressive drives, built in by evolution. They see anger as a reaction necessary for the human organism to survive life-and-death confrontations. (And we all know that one's child spilling milk at the dinner table is a life-and-death situation!)

Other people believe that sometimes we have control over our feeling of anger, though they tend to believe that what is more important is how we handle the anger. This is a view of anger popularly advanced by mental health therapists. The emotion of feeling anger is not something we can prevent if something external to us ignites it. It is as though anger is a program buried in our emotional computer, waiting for an outsider to key in the proper commands to call it up. Suppressing the feeling of anger is futile, since that bottled anger will escape anyway, if not at the moment of ignition, then later on, in another form and in other circumstances. Haven't we all snapped at our spouse or our children or our co-workers because the boss angered us earlier in the day?

What is important about feeling anger, say the therapists, is not so much the feeling itself, but that we vent that feeling fully, candidly, and in a nonviolent, socially acceptable manner. Punching someone in the face at the office or throwing a tantrum in the middle of the living room is normally not considered appropriate behavior. Standard advice is to count to ten, take your rage out on a punching bag, take a walk, or scream at a wall for several minutes.

While these psychological and evolutionary perspectives on anger are useful as background, what I am concerned about here is, do we or do we not have a choice in the first place whether we *experience* that feeling of anger? Let me reiterate what I mean by choice. Choice is not necessarily a matter of wanting or wishing or desiring, which is how choice is commonly defined. When I speak of choice, I mean the act of deciding or authoring or creating ownership of individual actions leading to a result—in this case, anger. Sometimes we make choices or decisions we do not want or wish, but we make the decisions nonetheless and we are responsible for them. Sometimes the decision is made unconsciously, as in a reaction; other times it is made consciously, alertly, with an understanding beforehand of the alternatives and consequences. We have and make choices in every now that we spend on this planet. It does not make any real difference whether we are conscious or not. We are still responsible.

The fact that two people often react to the same stimuli in different ways suggests that emotions are not something programmed into us, but we in fact choose how we will react or not react. That choice may be unconscious, it may surface quickly, but it is nevertheless a choice.

This matter of choosing or not choosing to feel a given emotion is not the distillation of a late-night college rap session over an esoteric metaphysical point from Psych 101. Understanding the true ownership of our emotions is fundamental to understanding and accepting personal responsibility and the sound management of ourselves. When you screamed at your daughter, "You make me so mad," you are relinquishing conscious control of your emotions. When we say "you let me down," "you disappointed me," "you make me happy," "you embarrassed me," we are attempting to pass responsibility for our own feelings and attitudes and consequential behavior onto someone else. We are allowing them to control our actions. We are playing from effect.

I write the word "shit." If you do not like that word, have I offended you? . . . Or have you chosen to be offended? If you say "You have offended me, Ted," that suggests I climbed inside your piece and told you what to think and what to feel. What you really mean is, that word is not acceptable to me and I have chosen to be offended. Or, I do not think that is an appropriate word, but I choose not to be offended.

Embarrassment. We've all got a few of those dumb embarrassing moments stashed away, don't we? Remember the day you split the seam out of your pants at high school or lost your car in the parking lot or forgot the name of someone you were about to introduce to a friend?

I was preparing to leave Denver one fine summer afternoon to fly to Miami for a seminar. I had my ticket in hand, my seat assignment, and my bags checked. I stopped off in the restroom and then headed down the concourse to Gate B-18 to catch the United flight. I soon spied walking the other way one of the most ravishing creatures I had ever seen. She was 5' 8," blond, and strutting along the concourse in a very tight pair of white shorts, open-toed high heels, and a pink halter top barely able to contain her large bazooms. I decided as I watched her approach that I was going to say "hi" when she passed me. The first thing I did, of course, was to suck in my belly (no small task) and when she was nearly aside me I tipped my head coolly and said, "Hi, how are you?" and she replied as she passed, "You better zip up, bud!"

Well, you can bet I chose to be embarrassed as everyone around us chuckled. I chose to turn 18 shades of red. Were there other choices? Yes, I could have remained cool and said, "I appreciate your interest," "Thanks for checking," or "Excuse me, I was just trolling." There were a number of options besides feeling embarrassed.

If you believe that other people *make* you embarrassed or mad or sad or happy, then you must believe that human beings are like automobiles in which anyone with a key or hot wire can climb inside you and drive off in any direction they wish. A silly analogy, right? Yet most of us think nothing of saying "He drives me crazy"—and believing it.

The Conditioning Excuse

When I suggest to people that we all are Charlie Browns playing the game of Life from effect instead of cause, their response is typically, "Well, Ted, what you say may be true, but we've been conditioned to respond this way. We've been taught to blame our bad results on others and only take credit for the good stuff. One can't change decades of conditioning overnight—if at all."

Nowhere are issues of choice and the conditioning of our behavior more hotly contested than on the subject of crime and criminals. Why does a person commit a crime? The answers we give to that question are profoundly important because they shape how we prevent crime and how we punish people who commit crimes. Moreover, the whole issue of the causes of crime spills over into other arenas of human relationships: if outside forces, physiological and psychological, "determine" how criminals behave then it is easier to use the same rationale in explaining our own noncriminal emotions and actions.

Like a pendulum, the theories of why a person robs or defrauds or murders others swing in one of two directions: environmental determinism or hereditary determinism. During the 1960's and 1970's, environmental determinism was in vogue. We experienced a high crime rate because criminals acted as they did because they suffered from poverty and unemployment, the baby boom, violence on television, child abuse and alcoholism, permissive parenting, racism, drug abuse, and poor cultural values, to name only a few. A criminal labeled with this kind of background was an individual seen as destined or condemned by upbringing and background, like a programmed rat, to commit crimes. "It wasn't his fault. Look at the conditions he grew up under."

In recent years, the pendulum has been swinging away from

this viewpoint toward the theory that some people are born with a physiological "predisposition" to crime. People commit crimes because they have suffered brain damage, have low IQ's, have a higher-than-average level of the male hormone testosterone, a lower-than-average level of an aggression-inhibiter chemical in the brain called serotonin, are more muscular, are suffering from premenstrual syndrome, or have a genetic predisposition because their parents were criminals. Drugs and physical environmental factors exacerbate these genetic factors in explaining why a given person commits a given crime.

Sometimes the physiological and psychological determinants are linked. Author Joe McGinniss, in his book, *Fatal Vision,* conjectures that Green Beret doctor Jeffrey MacDonald, convicted in 1979 of brutally murdering his wife and their two children, did so because (1) he felt psychologically threatened by his wife and (2) on the night of the murders he ingested an excessive amount of diet pills containing amphetamines. Don't most of us believe in our hearts that no person could really "be in his right mind" to murder someone?

What has been lost, or simply discounted, in this furious nature-versus-nurture debate, however, is the simple notion that while all these environmental and physiological factors may indeed tend to "predispose" someone to crime, the ultimate decision to commit a crime is a matter of free choice, or popularly called, free will. The fact is, people are damned tired of criminals making excuses and the courts letting them off because of those excuses.

To suppose that people can be explained as concretely and cleanly as one explains a thermonuclear reaction is to suppose we are mere animals. Certainly many scientists and philosophers hold that viewpoint. Yet if humans were merely a collection of chemicals and cells and a little wiring how could we also have two traits that most distinguish us from animals: the capacity for self-awareness and the capacity for abstract, conceptual thought? Humans are aware of themselves, their existence, and they can reason, a claim no other creature nor physical element on earth can make. The fact that you can sit here right now and contemplate choosing different ways to behave is proof that we all are products of our own choices.

While poverty, brain damage, alcohol, socially unacceptable friends, testosterone, and too much television all may be factors that predispose a given individual to crime or violence, no person can be explained simply by the sum of those parts. We are always more than that; if that were not the case, wouldn't all people who have experienced poverty, abusive parents, and are muscular males be criminals? Why do some people who experience those circumstances go on to be average or even exemplary citizens— working hard at a job, raising a family, being warm and loving individuals—while others rob banks and con old ladies out of their life savings? Why does a "nice" individual get along with his boss and fellow workers, yet at home beat his wife and kids? I contend it is a matter of choice, though often not a conscious choice, nor a simple matter. Past "conditioning" is difficult to overcome as one makes choices in present nows, though the fact is yesterday has nothing to do with today except to the extent that we choose to let it. American society sanctions wife and child abuse. Yet it disapproves, or at least does not condone as strongly, assaults on fellow employees. Anyone capable of distinguishing that difference is in effect "choosing" when to be violent and when not to.

Alcohol, drugs, and other chemicals do influence (but not determine) how the brain works and how we behave. But studies by such scientists as Samuel Yochelson and Stanton Samenow have shown that criminals can be taught to monitor their thoughts, to remain aware of who they are and what they are doing. Our ability to reason, to be aware of ourselves (some obviously more aware than others), to think conceptually, to examine our feelings and impulses, gives us an undeniable veto power over all those other forces. That veto power is choice.

Inconsistent Modeling

I think we have evolved as a species into this universal attitude of playing from effect, of finding excuses for our behavior, primarily because of inconsistent modeling. We have been taught and preached to since we were young that we are responsible for the choices that we make in our lives, though even that preaching has been watered down to some extent in recent years as more and more people look to others to take care of them.

Remember the saying made popular during the Vietnam War, "Suppose they gave a war and nobody came"? In that wonderfully cogent phrasing was conveyed the idea that war, despite the popular notion, is not something dictated by generals and presidents and the military-industrial complex. Wars are fought because individuals—each of us—*choose* to lace up our combat boots, shoulder our rifle, and trudge off to face death. This is not to argue that Vietnam or any other war should or should not have been fought. I am saying that wars are fought because individuals—not *a* nation or a group of individuals—*decide* to fight them (draft or no draft). War, like a brawl in a local bar, does not occur because it is "written on the wall" or as an inevitable consequence of the inescapable tides of history or as a conspiracy of military-industrial complexes or as a loose cabal of the rich and powerful. The 58,000 names etched in the black granite Vietnam Monument in Washington, D. C., the names of the men and women who died in the war, are there because each of those people chose to go to war and chose to die. One of those names belongs to my brother.

Unfortunately, our parents, our teachers, our heroes, our leaders, our politicians do not consistently follow their own admonitions. Any child with open eyes can see that—and a child's eyes are very open, for nobody lives in the present now more than children. Our role models pick and choose when they are going to be responsible and when somebody else or some other thing is going to be responsible. They bitch and blame when it suits them. Who the hell wants to be held responsible for the bad stuff?

The Why Game

One reason many of us have difficulty shaking off the paralyzing attitude of effect and taking responsibility for ourselves is that we get caught up in the Why Game. The Why Game is popular among therapists. You've heard the old joke about the person who asks the psychiatrist why she always answers every statement by her patients with a question. "Why do you ask?" she replies.

Now the Why Game can play a useful role in understanding and changing our behaviors and our attitudes. If we see the real reasons why we do some of the things we do, we can realize how silly or cruel or absurd the reasons are, decide the rationales behind our actions are not valid, and consequently change our behavior. Unfortunately, too many people play the Why Game to avoid changing their behavior. To use your past as an excuse for why you do not make more conscious choices in the present is fleeing from your sense of responsibility. Stop figuring out why and simply change your behavior. You may see the why later, which is fine, but change now.

Determining why I chose the nows I did in the past can be a valuable exercise as long as I use that information to help me choose more agreeable and conscious nows today and tomorrow. I would argue, of course, that all of us chose, if only unconsciously, to be conditioned to avoid responsibility in the first place. We are besieged by thousands of stimuli every now of our lives and we selectively choose which of those stimuli will have an impact on us.

Endless Choices

Changing 30 or 40 or 50 years of irresponsible habits is difficult. But if we allowed ourselves to be conditioned in the first place, then we can allow ourselves to unlearn those same habits, and much faster because we are conscious of making the changes. Habits are merely the accumulation of bits of behavior strung together, and bits of behavior can be changed. Each of us, in every now, has a series of alternatives, of choices, of how we will feel and behave. You can choose to get angry and throw this book in the trash, or you can choose to read on. You can decide to watch TV, open a bottle of fine wine, leap out of the chair and scream, make an obscene phone call to your neighbor with the dog that waters your flowers, demand a raise from your boss, or any of a thousand other choices.

With the recognition that we author our own feelings, that we alone are responsible for the choices of our nows, then the need to find excuses, to blame and find fault with others, evaporates. You cannot blame another person or the weather or the telephone if you acknowledge that it was your choice to feel that way or to put yourself in that particular situation. Your personal alternatives and options suddenly become endless.

If you approach life from this proactive attitude, then you will quickly discover that not only will you feel better about yourself because you are more in control of your own life, but you will find this has a curiously responsive effect on those around you. Are not your children or your partner or your friends apt to react more calmly when you are more calm? When you do not allow a disruptive situation to disrupt you, does that not have a calming effect on those around you? If you say to yourself, "I choose not to get angry at this situation," you will find that often the situation will resolve itself in a more agreeable manner. (We will explore this more in the chapter on reflection.)

Most of our misery occurs when we try to put the responsibility for our butt into someone else's hands, when we assume they are watching out for our best interests, when we allow external events to do things to us. Look at your own life. Look at the events that you did not like versus the ones that you did. Who was in control? Were not the events in which you took charge the ones that turned out the best for you?

"Results do not lie." Ask any parachutist who leaped without checking first.

You are the manager of a large department in a large corporation. Your department has a high turnover rate. Who is causing it to happen? The employees? Personnel? The boss above you?

The previous boss? Who picked them? Even if you were not the one who hired them, they are now part of your reality, and you are 100 percent responsible for everything that you experience in your reality. Are the people who are leaving doing it to you? Or are you allowing it to be done to you? Are you doing something about it, or are you making excuses?

In that same corporation, how many meetings have you gone to that do not start on time or should never have been called in the first place? How much time do you waste cleaning up after someone else who didn't finish his or her job properly?

On the planet Earth no one else ever does it to you. So why do you do that to you, Charlie Brown?

We must come to understand that every human being on this planet is the center of his or her own experiences, and they are 100 percent responsible for everything that they cause to happen to them. Until we can shift this universal attitude of effect over to cause, until we have everyone playing this game called Life by the same rules, we will continue to have a world in which nobody is in charge, in which no one cooperates, a world . . . like ours today.

Shifting that universal attitude does not mean trying to "fix" the other guy. What most of us want from other people is for them to always take total responsibility for managing their own lives. We want them to keep their agreements with us all of the time, we want them to tell the truth to us all of the time, we want them to not blame and find fault with others all of the time . . . Us? Oh, we'll do the best we can. And when we do not get it done, would everyone else please understand that we tried.

We all try, don't we? . . . I tried to get to work on time but the traffic was bad . . . I tried to write sooner but the kids keep me so busy . . . I try to be a calm, understanding parent, but my kids won't listen to me . . . Our marriage would have lasted but he would never compromise . . .

You say, "I should have." Notice you did not. "I could have." Notice you did not. "If only . . . " Notice you did not.

Trying only counts in rugby, horseshoes, darts, and purgatory. The rest is DDS—dog doo simple. You either step in it or you don't, and you know right away if you did or didn't, especially if you're barefoot.

I want you to try to put down this book. Think about what I am telling you. I do not *not* want you to put it down and I also do not want you to put it down. I want you to *try* to put it down.

"Try" to quit smoking. "Try" to loose weight.

You either produce results or you do not. Charlie Brown either succeeds in kicking the football or he fails. Trying does not score a field goal. His success or failure depends entirely upon him. There are no excuses, there are no in-betweens.

In life, results do not lie.

5

Memos from Uranus

TOP SECRET

TO: Chief Executive Officer Wynton Bernstein

FROM: Special Investigator Robert Martel

DATE: August 3, 2087

SUBJECT: Uranus subsidiary

I arrived yesterday at the Europa Station as scheduled. That new hyperdrive made the trip surprisingly fast. My cover as Galactic product manager for the company looks solid. I don't think anyone suspects I'm actually here on special investigation.

Uranus looks surprisingly similar to Earth. It is amazing how the TerraForm branch of the Interworld Federation of Civil Engineers has transformed this once harsh planet into a comfortable, beautiful land. However, despite the similarities, I sense that something is wrong on Uranus, though I can't quite put my finger on it yet.

During the flight I studied the reports about the problems at our subsidiary here. Very disturbing. I can appreciate your sense of urgency on this one, Mr. Bernstein. The drop in production, the cost overruns, the sloppy bookkeeping, the high rate of absenteeism and accidents, the mismanagement, the employee complaints—all are alarming, especially when compared to the excellent records of the other interworld subsidiaries of Galactic

General Corporation. I'll have a better handle on things in a few days.

TOP SECRET

TO: CEO Wynton Bernstein

FROM: Special Investigator Robert Martel

DATE: August 23, 2087

SUBJECT: Excuse making

Something is definitely wrong at our Uranian subsidiary; indeed, it is planet-wide, as I initially feared. I noticed it almost immediately, and in a highly unusual form: excuse making. Yes, that is correct, Mr. Bernstein, excuse making. I know it is difficult to believe, what with no excuses allowed on Earth or at any Galactic General Corporation interworld subsidiaries. But such is the case here.

At a production meeting this morning, the assistant production supervisor said her report would be late because several of the departments reporting to her had yet to provide the necessary information. And you know what, Chief? The production supervisor accepted that! He said he understood that since she was only 23 percent responsible for the project she could not be held totally accountable for getting her report in on time. Consequently, the subsidiary will delay start-up of its new mining operation until January. And worse, chief, I understand this was the third such delay in the last year. No wonder production schedules have slipped so drastically.

Speaking of excuses, most of the employees in my department are late to work every day, which they blame on the traffic and lack of adequate parking. When I tell them those are not excuses they look at me as though I am crazy. I recommend we immediately send an occupational health engineer up here to check out the company's environmental atmosphere.

Sickness is another severe problem here, Chief. Employees frequently miss work because they are sick. Worse, the company's management manual states that no employee will be held responsible for his or her being sick. And it is not only at this company, either. The entire planet of Uranus is a walking sick ward.

But the really shocking part is how they get sick. There are special fields on the outskirts of Europa Station where you can literally pick up bugs. I don't mean crickets or mosquitoes, chief; I mean cold bugs, flu bugs, hay fever, bronchitis, strep, pneumonia, cancer—you name it, they have a field for it. You just walk into the field of your choice and paw around in the grass until you find a bug, and then you swallow it. That's how you pick up bugs on Uranus.

Worse, here on Uranus people really care if you are sick. There's no better excuse going. Tell somebody here how sick you are or how tired you are or how your feet hurt, and the person will break down and cry and sympathize with you. It's enough to make you want to get sick all the time, which is what many Uranians do.

Remember the day I told you I had caught a flu bug from my kids and that I couldn't go on a mission? You looked at me and said, "Martel, try to imagine how little I care. Look deep into my eyes and see if you haven't mistaken me for someone who gives a hoot. No, excuses, remember? Choose not to get the flu in the first place. Take responsibility for yourself, Martel. Your kids didn't give you the flu; you took it."

TOP SECRET

TO: CEO Wynton Bernstein

FROM: Special Investigator Robert Martel

DATE: September 7, 2087

SUBJECT: Uranian Heights

I took a day off recently (I'd look suspicious, Chief, if I didn't) and hiked some of the beautiful mountains the TerraForm people have created here. Stunning vistas, deep gorges, towering peaks. Magnificent. Reminds me a lot of the Canadian Rockies before the Big War. I was nervous climbing some of the narrow trails. I've always been scared of heights on earth, but I always knew it was only in my head, that I chose to be afraid of high places. Heights don't care, right? But here on Uranus, Chief, heights really do scare you. I was hiking a rather narrow trail above timberline and all of a sudden the entire mountain went "Boo!" God, I've never heard anything like it! It sounded like a thousand thunderstorms rolled into one voice. Let me tell you, chief, it scared the hell out of me. My next day off I'm planning to stay a little closer to my apartment.

Which reminds me, Chief, I have moved out of the apartment you rented for me and into a brand new three-room home. I realize now that although you wanted a report in three Earth months, this is going to take longer than we planned.

TOP SECRET

TO: CEO Wynton Bernstein

FROM: Special Investigator Robert Martel

DATE: September 29, 2087

SUBJECT: Feeling Hurters

I'm experiencing increasing doubts about the risks of this assignment, Chief. Per your instructions, I have confronted in private several Galactic managers about some of the inexcusable excuses I've witnessed to date. I did not tell them I was speaking for you, of course; just my private observations, I told them. You know what they did to me, Chief? They hurt my feelings!

I realize that back home nobody can hurt my feelings. I may allow somebody to hurt them, when I choose to value what someone else says about me more than what I know to be true. It's my choice. But on Uranus they can hurt your feelings without your acceptance of it. The reason they can is that everyone carries a funny little beeper-like device—you know, like the pagers the neurotics carry at home—that they can aim at you and zap your feelings. I mean, these managers said I was being unkind in my accusations, and then they aimed their beepers at me, dialed in the proper feeling, and *made* me feel like a heel. I think I need help on this assignment, Chief, and to hell with the security risks.

TOP SECRET

TO: CEO Wynton Bernstein

FROM: Special Investigator Robert Martel

DATE: October 15, 2087

SUBJECT: Guilt

Sorry I'm so late getting this report to you, Chief. I don't know what's come over me these days. I'm not a church goer, as you know, but out of curiosity I attended our Lady of Perpetual Sorrow and Guilt Forever, which is a huge edifice in the center of Europa Station, and frankly, I haven't felt the same since I left that place. I've had this nagging sense of guilt ever since. I know that's crazy, because I know that on Earth guilt is a wasted emotion and a waste of time; worrying about what happened yesterday won't change yesterday or the situation today. If you're feeling guilty about your past nows you can't be living in the present and making wise choices about your current nows.

Still, I cannot seem to shake these guilty feelings, and that's really bothering me. But I'm not alone. The Uranians thrive on guilt. You'll be cruising on the PeopleMover and all of a sudden the person in front of you will bend down and begin petting some ugly, hairy little creature that's sucked onto the person's ankles. The first time I saw that I asked the person what the hell the thing was and he said, "It's a *chuca*."

"God, that looks disgusting," I said. "What's a *chuca*?"

He looked surprised, until I explained that this was my first visit to Uranus. So he explained that a "*chuca* senses when you're feeling guilty about something and when it does it sucks your ankle."

"So why are you petting it?" I stupidly asked.

"Because I'm feeling guilty, of course."

Uranians take their guilt seriously, too, Chief. They have Guilt Groups all over the Station on the weekends. I stumbled into one one evening quite by accident. I saw a notice for a Thirty

Years' War group. I've always been fascinated by military history, so I went thinking it was some kind of lecture. Instead, I found 300 Uranians gathered in a big circle listening to an elderly man in the center of the circle reciting a long list of German names. I asked what was going on and someone said everyone was feeling guilty for the people who had died in the Thirty Years' War. Now if I recall correctly, the Thirty Years' War occurred on Earth in the early 1600's, but here were these people wallowing in guilt about the deaths of Otto and Hans and Frederick and Johann and Karl and a bunch of other long-dead Germans. Come to find out, there are Guilt Groups about the starving on Venus, the pollution on Io, the crime on Jupiter, and the racism in the Nova Galaxy, to name only a few.

What's stranger, Chief, is that on Uranus feeling guilty actually does make a difference. I talked to a man who lives next door and he told me that several years ago he and his wife had gotten divorced. He said he had felt terribly guilty about it because he knew the breakup was really his fault, and he felt terrible about leaving his kids and the family dog. Now we both know, chief, that back home this man was 100 percent responsible for experiencing that divorce. So were his wife and kids. But that does not mean he should have felt guilty. Rather, he should have learned from his experience and used that knowledge in his present nows to get on with living. Not this man. He whined and moaned about it so much, and he attended so many Divorce Guilt Groups and petted so many *chucas* that his wife and kids actually took him back. Of course, now he feels guilty that he has not been fair to himself—I mean, the man still doesn't get along with his wife—but that's another story.

I also have caught wind of some Worry Groups—people who worry about the future even though it hasn't gotten here yet. It's very mystical and very secretive, I'm told, because allegedly their worrying about tomorrow can actually change the future. I'm anxious to learn more about them.

All this is no lie, Chief. I realize you may think I'm making all this up. But *chucas* and Guilt Groups and Our Lady of Perpetual Sorry and Guilt Forever really do exist on Uranus. I tell you, Chief, this planet is driving me crazy.

TOP SECRET

TO: CEO Wynton Bernstein

FROM: Special Investigator Robert Martel

DATE: November 21, 2087

SUBJECT: Complexes and Phobias

It's been a while since my last report, I know, but let me assure you I'm still hard at work on this case. Let me cite what happened yesterday, which I really should have spotted sooner. As our top-secret company reports indicated, this subsidiary is plagued by an alarmingly high rate of absenteeism and on-the-job accidents. Part of that is due to the plague of illnesses among employees, but I've also noticed that many of the employees here suffer from a variety of complexes and phobias. Yesterday I tracked down the source.

I accompanied several fellow employees to a nearby 7–12 store during a morning break. Northland Corp. certainly has cornered the market here. Anyway, we went back into a corner of the store where a large bright red display case stood that advertised phobias and complexes. Just so as not to arouse any suspicions, I bought a few things myself, which I investigated more thoroughly after I got home. It's astounding, Chief. One item I had purchased was an economy-size box of Ailurophobia (that's fear of cats, you know), put out by BioMind Laboratories, for the mere cost of one Imperial crown. Another was a small tin of Xenophobia. Both are powders you mix in milk. I had passed up containers of Astrophobia, Agoraphobia, and Bulimia. The pills were even more amazing. I've bought Vitamin A and Vitamin B Complex in London, Chief, but I don't ever remember seeing pills for Inferiority Complex, Persecution Complex, Obsessive-Compulsiveness, Shyness, Passive-Aggressiveness, Stress, Hypochondria, Alcoholism, Paranoia, Depression, and Infantilism. You can also buy powders and pills for Elation, Happiness, Cheerfulness, Extroversion, Assertiveness, and Health, but my fellow employees seemed to ignore that section. I've sampled the contents of some of the powders and pills, and the damn stuff works. Last night I went downtown and found I couldn't go near a cat—and I love cats.

This place is really weird, Chief. And I'm worried they're on to me.

TOP SECRET

TO: Wynton

FROM: Special Investigator Robert Martel

DATE: December 19, 2087

SUBJECT: Anxiety Attacks

I appreciate the concern you expressed in your last message, Chief. I know I'm not functioning as well as I have on past assignments. Remember how I uncovered that mismanagement and corruption in our Venusian subsidiary? But here on Uranus I'm no longer sure about how much longer I can carry out this mission. As the holidays approach, I've found myself suffering frequently from anxiety attacks. I know what you're saying, Chief. Anxiety doesn't attack on Earth. You allow anxiety and stress to affect you because you are unsure of yourself or what you are doing in your now. But I tell you, Chief, anxiety really does attack here on Uranus. It comes down from the hills surrounding Europa Station—a bunch of A's and X's and N's who ride in packs on horseback and attack people with bullwhips and piercing yells. It was the most terrifying experience I have ever felt.

Another strange occurrence recently has also upset me. As you know, I'm not one to let my videophone interfere with my work. People can only call me at certain times of the day and that's it. But the other afternoon, during one of my quiet periods when I was doing paperwork, my videophone started making funny sounds, flickering the screen off and on, ringing even though I had put all calls on the message tape. I called in a repairperson and she told me right away what the problem was: I wasn't using the videophone enough. It knows when I'm in the room and if I don't use it while I'm there it feels very hurt. So said this repairperson. She said I needed to think of the videophone as a child, not an inanimate object.

Chief, these people here on Uranus are nuts!

TOP SECRET

TO: Wynton

FROM: Special Investigator Robert Martel

DATE: February 9, 2088

SUBJECT: Life Does It To You

Sorry I'm late getting back to you, Chief. I've got several of your messages piled up here on my desk. How long has it been since I last reported? I've lost track of time. It's difficult getting my reports transmitted now because the Comm Division is so disorganized. Plus, I've had a severe case of Uranian viral flu for weeks, and for two days I couldn't even get to work because my Hovermobile wouldn't start.

But I have to say, Chief, I think I've finally figured out why things run the way they do on Uranus. Yesterday I stopped by a small bookstore located just back of Our Lady of Perpetual Sorrow and Guilt Forever. Naturally, there was a long line of Uranians there so I got in line and waited forever (there was just one clerk and she didn't seem to know how to work the credit card machine) to see what they were buying. When I got to the counter the girl handed a little red book to me and charged me four Imperial crowns for it. I didn't get a good look at it until I got home last night. The book is called *Life Does It To You.* I haven't finished reading it, but what I have read is quite fascinating. I don't know yet who wrote it. I've noticed not only at work but everywhere on Uranus that nobody takes credit for authoring anything. As soon as I finish the book, Chief, I'll write my final report.

Life is a game of tag, and you're always it.

6

Hellooooo, Anybody Home?

Life is not a money-back proposition. If you do not like some of the individual "nows" you experience in your life, you do not get to return them to the customer service counter for a refund. Each now occurs once and only once, and you get to keep it, good or bad. So it is obvious that the way to get the most from your life is to get the most out of each of those nows. After all, if you are already totally responsible for your nows, you might as well make the choices that you want or desire, as opposed to the ones you don't want. When you played from effect, when you believed that others were making choices for you, then you tended to accept the bad things because they were "their fault" or "that's life" or "Some days you eat the bear and some days the bear eats you." But if you are making the choices, why would you want the bear to eat you?

One way to improve the quality of those nows is to be conscious when you have them. We're not on this planet for very long so why not be present for it?

I've noticed when I look around me that a lot of people don't spend much time being home. What I mean by being home or conscious or aware or living in the present, is when your mind and your body are in the same place at the same time. Your mental awareness and your physical being are in the same *now*.

So where is *now*? I like to illustrate where now is by asking someone to sit in a chair, close his or her eyes, and recall the person's high school days. Think of his favorite class, her favorite teacher. What was the teacher's name? What did the room look like, what did the participant like most about class? While the person is fondly recalling these memories, I'll pick up a large pitcher or glass of ice water, and stand behind the participant. I rattle the ice and ask the people around me: "If I pour this pitcher of water over this person's head, where will the person get wet . . . here or back in the high school classroom?"

The question usually evokes a quick response by the person in the chair. Obviously, "here" is where your physical body is. Home is always where your piece is. When your mind and physical body are split, when your physical being is in the *now* and your mental awareness is in the past or in the future or lost in transit, that is called not being conscious. You are being unconscious, or *unc*. I abbreviate the word unconscious to *unc* because it beats the hell out of daydreaming.

Look at the tattoos on your body—your scars. I would wager that you got most of them when you were *unc*. You weren't home when you got them, though you quickly came home once you did get them. Accidents do not happen . . . they are caused.

I recall coming back one day from Newport Beach, California, after conducting one of my three-day seminars. I was puttering around in my garage, trying to unwind, going unconscious or *unc*, when my daughter Megan came in to talk to me about something. She's talking and I'm puttering around and not listening and she finally says, "Sometimes when you get home, dad, you're not home."

Signs of Unc

We know we're not home or living in the now, we know our mind and our body are in two different places at the same time, when we:

Walk into the wrong restroom.
Put the ice cream away in the refrigerator.
Drive past our turnoff to work.
Pull like hell when the door says PUSH.
Get off the elevator on the wrong floor.
Lock our keys in the car.
Sit down on the toilet in the middle of the night
with the seat up.

70

Leave the iron on.

Answer a question not asked.

Hit our thumb with a hammer.

Look for our car on Level 3 when it is parked on Level 4.

You can usually tell when someone has gone *unc* on you. Check into a hotel and the front desk clerk is never home. If you find one that is home, the hotel probably does more business than anyone else in the state. You approach the desk and give your name to the clerk. Seconds later this same clerk will ask, "What's your name?" If you ask a question or leave instructions, the clerk will study your ear with glazed eyes and an absent nod. It makes you want to lean across the desk and yell, "Hellooooo, anyone home?"

Next time you fly, watch how many people are *unc*. The flight attendants are rattling off safety instructions that could, in the event of a real emergency, save lives ("In the event of the sudden loss in cabin pressure an oxygen mask will automatically drop down in front of you. Take the mask . . . ") But is anybody paying attention? The business people are already deep into their *Wall Street Journals*, parents are struggling to strap their kids in, and the remainder are asleep.

The only people conscious are new fliers. During one flight I listened to a flight attendant break into the following nonsense ("In the event of the sudden loss in cabin pressure a chicken will drop down in front of you. Put your lips to the chicken's lips and . . . "). I don't think two heads turned. During another flight a pilot joked over the intercom, "We'll leave the gate as soon as the flight attendants clear the aisles so I can see out the back window." Three people laughed.

Who isn't home in your life? Probably your kids. Your boss or fellow employees. The gas station attendant. The people you meet at parties who can't remember your name three seconds after you introduce yourself. The clerk at the grocery store. Your spouse or partner.

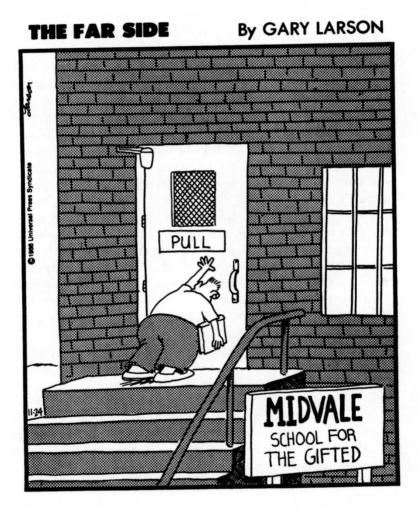

THE FAR SIDE COPYRIGHT 1986
UNIVERSAL PRESS SYNDICATE
Reprinted with permission. All rights reserved.

Spouses are rarely home for each other, especially the longer they've been married. They figure that after so many years they've heard every original thought the other person has to say, so there's not much point in listening anymore. This can be disconcerting, however, not only to your spouse but to you.

"Did you bring home the TV from the repair shop, dear?" your spouse asks. *"Gone with the Wind* is on tonight."

"Oh, shit," you say, a phrase your spouse has definitely heard before. "I thought you were going to do that."

"No, I couldn't. Last night I asked you to pick it up this afternoon on your way home from work because I had a doctor's appointment. You said you would."

"I did? I didn't hear you."

"That's because you were reading the paper instead of listening."

Sex therapists Masters and Johnson claimed in a study that 87 percent of the people who make love are not home for their partner. How they determined this, I don't know, but the numbers illustrate how little we are home, even for something you would think most people would be home for.

Don't get me wrong. Being *unc* can be beneficial. Some of our most creative moments, our planning times, our forecasting times occur when we are unconscious. Watching television is often a great time to leave home. So is sitting in the bathroom or listening to a politician speak.

The problems begin to occur when we go *unc* at moments we don't want to or shouldn't. When you drove to work this week, how many people did you see picking their noses or singing, talking to themselves, shaving, reading a book, or putting on makeup while they were driving? That is not, in my estimation, a smart time to leave the present moment.

How often have you read about athletes who said, after suffering an ignominious defeat, "I just wasn't in the game"? Translated, that means, "I wasn't home, I had my mind elsewhere while my body was on the field." How often are our children's' minds somewhere other than focused on what the teacher just wrote on the blackboard?

Being Unc *from Responsibility*

Being unconscious is a major reason people today have a tough time taking personal responsibility for the consequences in their lives. The only times you can produce results in your life are in the present moments. If you are *unc* during most of your nows, the only thing you are going to produce is excuses.

Little wonder two thirds of the people who get married get divorced. They aren't home for each other most of the time.

Little wonder our relationships with our children are often shrill or empty. We're not home for them when they are telling us about problems they're having in school or about how they're feeling depressed and suicidal.

Little wonder so many workers injure themselves on the job. (Of course, they rarely hold themselves responsible; it's easier to sue the company for not having 55 orange Day-glo safety signs plastered on the piece of machinery.)

Little wonder tens of thousands of people die on our nation's highways each year. Do they die because they aren't wearing their seat belts or the cars aren't well built? No, most die because they choose not to have their minds on the road, where their bodies are.

Little wonder so many of us don't seem to enjoy life as much as we think we should. We're never home for it.

We go to a party full of friends, yet we end up dwelling on why the big sales meeting last week didn't go well or the fact the roof needs fixing tomorrow or on how we'd loved to go to a baseball game next Saturday if only we had more time. After we get home from the party we wonder why we didn't have much fun.

When do you think you first went *unc*? When was the first time you slipped out of the present and into the unconscious? Let's go back to your early days, say just prior to your birth. Remember what the conditions were back then? Warm, 98.6°, your own private pool where you could do a few laps, dark, quiet except for a comforting heartbeat, lots of food prepared by mom, mom breathing for you—your own private "womb service."

Then comes birth.

All of a sudden it's crowded in there. Hey, who the hell drained my pool? You want me to go through there? No way! Suddenly you're out, unceremoniously dropped into the hands of Johnny Bench. You have a headache a bottle of aspirin wouldn't lick. Bright lights. Cold. Noisy. Dry. Fear. A slap on the butt, and if you are a boy you get a special added attraction. Now you've got to order food and drink. No wonder the only thing you want to do is crawl back into where you've been the last nine months. Only the door's closed. And for many of us, we spend the rest of our life trying to get back into that womb by going *unc*.

Cinnamon Rolls and Watches

The way we do that is often subtle and unconscious. The next time you're in a meeting or at a party watch how many distractions people create for themselves, some intentional some not, to avoid interacting with others around them.

Drinking cups of coffee or booze, glancing at watches to see how soon it is to lunch time, smoking, and making designs out of napkins are popular. But if they're slurping at a cup of coffee or staring at their watch, how can they be conscious for whoever they are talking or listening to?

Food is the same way. How conscious are you going to be at an important business meeting if you are drooling over a cinnamon roll sitting in front of you? Let's make it a cinnamon roll that overflows the plate. It is so hot steam is rolling across the top of it and the icing is oozing down the sides. You stare ravenously as two patties of *real* butter slowly melt into a pool atop the roll. You begin to tear off pieces and stuff them into your mouth and savor their deliciousness. Now, what did your boss just say the last few minutes while you were stuffing your face?

Smoking's a good way to escape, too. In graduate school I would sit in class in the same chair every time (if someone else got there first it ruined my whole day) while some guy up front did his dog and pony show. I'd sit there and drag on my cigarette and blow smoke rings. I got so good I could blow itty bitty rings *inside* a larger one. I even got the students around me to watch. Who was home for this professor?

Don't we stumble through life separated from our nows by one distraction after another, trying to do six things at a time? We carry on conversations while one eye is on the television, we negotiate business deals while stuffing our faces with Crab Louie and martinis, we write bills while talking long distance with a friend. No wonder we make mistakes or can't recall later what was said. (If you're reading this book while the television is on you're either missing some of what I'm saying or you are finding yourself rereading portions because you saw the words but not the content the first time through.)

Not that anything is wrong with each of these things in themselves—the television doesn't care whether it is on or off. But it does matter when we let them distract us from being in the now, from maintaining eye contact, from listening and concentrating, from being productive.

We so overschedule events in our lives—aerobic workout to the grocery store to a movie to a fast food joint to the airport—that our mind never seems to catch up with our physical being. While we're at aerobics we're thinking about the movie, but when we're at the movie we're thinking about a report that's due tomorrow, and while we're stuffing down a hamburger we're jotting down an itinerary for next week. And somewhere in there a new 15-story building popped up and we're wondering where it came from. They must have moved that sucker in by truck last night.

Individual responsibility means producing results *now*. How can you make sound, rational, conscious choices about your present actions if you're not producing those results in the present? It is important to learn from the past and plan or anticipate tomorrow. However, results must be produced in the now.

We're Home Less These Days

Most of us spend less and less time in our nows as we get older, until we face death or any shock about our physical well being. Death invariably sharpens the present for people. Ask people who have experienced a life-threatening situation and they will tell you they were acutely aware of every single moment, everything that was going on around them. "I was only on that hijacked airplane for twelve hours . . . but it seemed like a week!" Or a friend or relative dies and suddenly you're acutely conscious of how precious each moment is.

My experience has been that the last time most of us were home for any length of time was when we were kids. Not in school, of course, or for our parents, but all the other times. Remember?

Let's do a little exercise. Imagine that time in your life when you were ten years old. Roll back those memory banks to then. Let's make it the middle of summer. Remember where you were living? It's early evening and you've eaten supper and you're out with your friends. You can hear the crickets and the sky is a soft, deep blue and the fireflies are beginning to come out.

What kind of games are you playing? Riding bikes? Hide-'n-go-seek? Dirt clod wars? Dolls? Those were always fun. Marbles? Shooting those aggies and steelies and cat's-eyes? Playing cowboys and Indians? Jacks? Red rover? Red light, green light? A little doctor if you could get away with it? Kick the can?

Kick the can was big in my town. I was born in Dover, New Hampshire, and raised in another small town, Springvale, Maine. We used to play kick the can a lot in Springvale. Of course, what can would you use but a Campbell's soup can. Any favorites? Mine was the tomato soup can. Maybe the chicken noodle was yours. The oldest can I remember using was a Pet Milk can.

We played kick the can for hours. We'd be out there playing until it was pitch black and my father would whistle for me. Remember those summer nights? Now I want to ask you an important question. Remember how long those nights were? Didn't it seem we had . . . forever?

When my kids were younger, the first thing they asked when they got out of school in June was, "When do we have to go back?" I'd explain that we were taking a vacation the latter part of June and we were going to Santa Fe for the fiesta around Labor Day, and that's when they'd go back to school, right after we get back from Santa Fe.

"That long!" they would say.

As adults, what are our summers like? When it's Labor Day, we're saying, "Where the hell did the summer go? Labor Day? I don't even remember the Fourth."

So what happened to all the time we had as kids? Were we issued bonus time back then, say 28 hours in a day instead of 24? When did we start to lose all that extra time? When we left home? When we started our families? When we took on more responsibilities? Why does life feel like it's passing us by, that we only have 18 hours in the day instead of 24?

Now from my understanding of physics, we still have the same amount of time each day as adults as we did as kids, give or take some microseconds for adjustments in the earth's rate of spin—that is, we have all the time there is. I also understand that where I live we have the same 24 hours you do where you live. So why do people keep telling me they "don't have as much time" as they used to?

It gets back to the fact that the older we get the less and less time we spend living in the present moment, less and less time in our nows. If we're not home to fully experience our nows— which we did as kids chasing leaves and making mud pies—no wonder we mumble about where they went.

One reason we're home less as we get older is we are afflicted with what I call *yamma yamma. Yamma yamma* is mind chatter. It is your mind always anticipating the next now . . . the next now . . . the next now—never being satisfied with the now you are in. Or thinking about past nows. Sometimes the *yamma yamma* is a whisper, other times a yell, but it is always going. It is always in the back of your mind racing all the time.

You're at another one of those interminable management

meetings, and while someone else is talking your mind is going "This is dumb . . . how long is this going to last? . . . I have to go to the bathroom . . . did I leave the lights on at home? . . . I've got to remember to pick Bill up after work . . . I wish I had gone to that play last week with Sally . . ." Haven't we all got one of those hummers? And as you get older your *yamma yamma* speeds up, like a 33 rpm record playing at 78 rpms. Ever lie in bed wanting to go to sleep, yet you can't shut that damn thing off?

Why this incessant self-talk? Why this avoidance of our present moments? Because it's safer. People often are not conscious or aware or alert because it is risky to be in the present. They are afraid of their own thoughts and feelings. They are afraid when they are home they'll find the house is empty. They are afraid they will have to produce. I'm sure that at work you know employees who are always busy, but never productive. They're always *telling* you how busy they are, yet they never seem to accomplish anything. They've got a *yamma yamma* that runs at 110 rpms. They're always in the next now. They're so busy in their mind going over all the activities they've got to accomplish they never accomplish anything. They're never conscious long enough to start or finish anything.

We learn as we get older that we should never be satisfied with the moment we're in. We should always be better, constantly growing, never content. What if something happens we didn't *yamma yamma* or think about?

How to Live More in the Present

If you want to learn to spend more time in the present, more time enjoying your nows, more time having productive instead of merely busy nows, slow down your *yamma yamma*. Slow down your *yamma yamma* and you "slow down" your life. Focus on what you are doing *now*. Eliminate distractions. Refuse to give in to distractions. Ever notice among your friends that the happiest ones are the ones who live the most in the "now"? Think of your friends and acquaintances. Think of the ones who are always worrying about tomorrow, about how much work they have to do or about some event (there is always some event) coming up that has them preoccupied. Or think of the ones who live mostly in the past, the good old days or the guilts they have about what they did or did not do yesterday. Are they as happy, as much fun, as productive and stimulating as your friends who live today?

Tomorrow I want you to spend a day in which you focus only on what you are doing, not what you did today or what you need or want to do the next day. Focus on each now. Make it the best now you can have. Do that for each now of the entire day. At the end of the day sit in a comfortable chair and reflect. Did the day seem longer than the days usually have been for you lately? Even if the day was packed with meetings and trips and chores, did you still feel the day didn't fly by so fast? Did you find the chores you hated to do actually took less time than they normally do because you worked more productively? Were you more efficient and more effective because you focused on each now? Did you accomplish what you wanted to do in that now and move onto the next now without dragging the past now with you or worrying about a future now?

Try this exercise for one day. And if one day sounds like too much, try it for only a few hours. Heaven knows I don't want you staying home too much at first. Moving back in should be a gradual process, getting the furniture put in the right place and the pictures up on the wall and generally making the place comfy to live in. Moving in to live 24 hours a day cold turkey may be too much of a shock for the system.

Our goal is, in the words of Baba Ram Dass, to "be here now." When is the only time in life you produce maximum results?

Now.

When is the only time you clean up that mess in your life?

Now.

You are totally responsible for the experiences of your life. If you are unhappy in your marriage, who is responsible for staying? Who is responsible for not changing the atmosphere of the relationship or seeking a way out of the relationship? The same

80

goes for a job you hate. If you don't like those experiences, change them. How can you change them? By realizing it is your choice and by living more in the present. When can you change them?

Now.

If you want to go *unc*, be consciously responsible for it. I remember more than once in my life sitting in a bar listening to a friend, and suddenly a lovely lady would pass and my eyes would wander from my friend's eyes and I would go *unc* to my friend's conversation. Now I say to my friend, "Wait a minute." I watch the girl go by and then I say to my friend, "I'm back. Go on." It is so much easier authoring the responsibility for going *unc*.

A Few Games

A fun way to get yourself, and others, into the now is to play a few mind games. They take a little risk on your part, but they bring you and those around you home real quick.

You're walking down the hallway and a fellow employee passes and says, "Hi, how are you?" To which you reply, "Hey, I appreciate your interest . . . [pause] . . . I'm having a good day, thanks." The reply completely throws their timing off because by then they are already down the hall when it dawns on them that things didn't go according to ritual. Or if you really want to get their attention, try, "Fine. My dog just died."

At a cocktail party one way to get good eye contact, to get the person you're talking to back home from the bean dip, is to give nonstandard answers to standard questions.

"Hi, what's your name?"

Richard Nixon.

"What do you do?"

I'm an oceanographer. I work in Phoenix.

"What's your sign?"

Yield.

"What's your birth order?"

I was out of order.

81

Use your imagination. Corny or witty, at least your replies will get them and you home.

If you really like to take risks, try introducing people to each other in elevators, or stand with your back to the elevator door. Walk down a hotel hallway and say to a total stranger, "Hi, how are you. How you been? Take care. Listen, talk to you later." You'll have that person wondering the rest of the day where he or she met you. And when you check into that hotel and the clerk behind the desk is having a bad day and is obviously *unc* and is treating you badly, just quietly lean over the counter and say softly, "Excuse me. Is anybody home?"

I tried to catch a cold
As he went running past
On a damp and chilly
Afternoon in autumn
I tried to catch a cold,
But he skittered by so fast
That I missed him—
But I'm glad to hear you caught him.
—Shel Silverstein

Reprinted by permission of Harper & Row, Publishers, Inc.

7

Mind, Body, and Spirit

Everyone on the planet Earth has a terminal disease.
It's called Life.

Nobody—at least, nobody I've met so far—has gotten off this planet alive. Yet most people sleepwalk through life instead of smelling the flowers. Woody Allen once remarked that "ninety percent of life is just showing up." That's what most people do—just show up. They exist instead of living fully or going for it. If you had 24 hours to live, what would you be doing right now? Yeah, me too. Now that we've got that settled, why aren't we doing it? Why aren't we living life as though we've only got 24 hours left? Why does it take a death in the family or a personal brush with death to rattle our cage about the priorities of life? Whether you are a believer in some sort of hereafter and that life on earth is just a quick stop at the gas station, or that with death you dissolve into nothingness, don't you owe it to yourself to live fully and not merely exist while you're spending time here?

I think one reason is we are confused about who we are. We think we are something different than who we really are. Who you are is really very simple.

You are.

Or from your perspective, I am.

"I am" is your essence, your soul, your spirit, The Force, your being—call it what you like. Now this is nothing new. I'm not going to pretend I dreamed that up or got it from my neighborhood Oracle. It is an ancient and often-debated view of life, and not a provable view at that. We will explore it more in the chapters on "The Truth Seeker" and "The Artichoke Syndrome." But for now, let's accept the notion that you know you are, that you exist, that you are the only person you have complete responsibility for, and that you are the product of the decisions you make in your life.

What is important to grasp here is you are your essence or your soul, but you are not your body or your mind. People are always getting that confused. They think of themselves as their body or their mind, and they let their mind or their body run them. But your body and your mind are merely tools to use to choose the best nows that your essence wants.

Fat Chance

It took me a while to understand this concept. Take being fat. I am what you might politely describe as well-fed. My idea of a good time is grazing over four fried chickens. I have always been this way and for most of my life I knew exactly who to blame: my mother. She *caused* me to be heavy:

It is in my genes.
I am big boned.
I am short.
My metabolism is out of whack.
I have a thyroid condition.
I love my mom.
People are starving in China.

The last one was always one of my favorites. "Do you know how many people are dying of starvation in China?" my mother would say whenever she caught me trying to hide my broccoli under the edge of my plate. I listened to that one for 18 years. I blamed my fatness on those mysterious Chinese. Until one day I said to her, "Mom, name me two."

At our house, love and food were wired together. We ate because we were happy, we ate because we were sad. We ate to show our love to mother. I used to look forward to funerals because the neighbors always brought in loads of great food. Food did it to me too. The damn mashed potatoes drowning in all that greasy gravy just jumped right off the plate and sucked my hip. The apple pie used to crawl off the plate and clamp itself to my stomach like a leech.

It took me years before I realized food had nothing to do with it. If it did, it would do it to all of us. The fact is, food does not care. I am heavy because I have been too lazy to exercise and too undisciplined to cut back on the fine wines and rich foods I so dearly love. I have been unwilling to take the responsibility to be thin. I have made the choice to be well-fed, and thus the health risks associated with being overweight.

As we explored in earlier chapters, the same excuse-making occurs when we blame our bodies for our behavior. Criminals are people led astray by short-circuited wiring in their brains, chemical imbalances, genetics. New studies show that genetics play a role in behavior such as shyness or aggressiveness. One recent study suggested that alcoholics become addicted to liquor because they are born with nervous systems more susceptible to dependency on alcohol. As with being fat, we tend to blame our condition on our body. We confuse our body with our soul, our potential, our essence. Yet we know alcoholism can be overcome, aggressiveness reduced, shyness mitigated.

You Are Not Your Piece

A lot of men and some women came back from Vietnam missing parts of their body. They checked into their local Veterans Administration hospital and proceeded to vegetate. They believed they were their piece, their physical being. And since their piece was damaged, they perceived they must themselves be damaged, their quality of life damaged.

Then there were returning vets who believed "they were" *and* they had a body. Max Cleland went to Vietnam as a member of the Marine Corps, Forced Recon. He went to Vietnam in 1967 standing 6'4" and came back 3'2" because he threw himself on a grenade and blew away both legs and one arm. Did Max Cleland let his body do it do him? No. Cleland subsequently served two terms in the Georgia Senate, became a staff member of the U. S. Senate Veterans' Affairs Committee in Washington, and in 1977 he became head of the VA under President Carter, the first Vietnam vet and the first amputee to do so.

I love to ski. One of the joys of my life is cruising the back bowls of Aspen and Vail, cutting through pristine early-morning powder. So it is with special affection and joy I've watched "handicapped" children and adults ski. At a Colorado ski resort named Winter Park, a special program was developed many years ago to teach handicapped people how to ski. These people are missing arms or legs. Many are paraplegic. Some are blind. Yet they not only ski, they ski *well*. Are they their bodies?

Each year nearly half a million people in the United States succumb to the Big C. Another million new cases are reported each year. Did these people have a choice? Did they cause themselves to experience cancer? Every year doctors tell thousands of sick patients, "You are going to be dead in six months." In one week, they buy the farm. They believed they were their bodies, and consequently what the doctors told them must be true.

Alabama football coach Bear Bryant predicted he would be dead within a month after he quit coaching. He did it in 28 days (and not by suicide). His wife had made statements that she could not live without him, and she died soon after he did. "Died of a broken heart" can be more than a poetic platitude.

On the other hand, how often have you heard of people who went to their doctor, received the same diagnosis, and said, "Thanks for the information, doc. I appreciate you sharing that with me. But I choose not to go yet. I'll let you know when I'm checking out." They proceeded to live years beyond the doctor's prognosis. Was the doctor wrong? Probably not. The patients merely decided to take 100 percent responsibility for their piece, not the other way around. They, along with people who have "miraculously" survived traumatic injuries, have what we often describe as "a strong will to live."

Byron Janis is a world-acclaimed concert pianist, considered by some as the world's greatest interpreter of Chopin's music. Yet Janis cannot make a fist, motion is severely limited in his right wrist, and the joints of most of his fingers are fused. Janis suffers, and has suffered for over a decade, from the "debilitating" disease of psoratic arthritis, a disease that would lead most pianists, amateur or professional, to abandon the keyboards. For several years Janis continued a heavy concert schedule despite the pain of practice and the difficulty in maintaining his skills. But by 1984, even the determined Janis found himself unable to play, though only his wife and he knew why. He clung to his secret, quit performing—a life he had known since he was a youngster—and withdrew into depression.

Nearly 36 million Americans suffer from psoratic arthritis, and most, when they reach the state Janis did, give up their daily lives, give in to the pain and the crippling of their bodies. They confuse their spirit with their bodies. Not Janis. When he quit playing, he also quit taking the painkillers, anti-inflammatory drugs, and tranquilizers he had mixed in his body to keep himself propped up for his concerts. But with the drugs gone, Janis found himself rediscovering his emotions, and dealing with them. As he later told *Parade* magazine, "The first thing I had to conquer was fear. I realized what a debilitating thing fear is. It can render you absolutely helpless. I know now that fear breeds fear. *If you think something terrible is going to happen, it frequently does.*" [my emphasis]

What Janis told himself was that, yes, he had arthritis, but there was still so much of life. With renewed intensity, Janis sought a variety of treatments for his condition, all of them drug-free. Gradually Janis began to play again, better than ever. In 1985, he became the National Arthritis Foundation's Ambassador for the Arts. As Janis said in the *Parade* magazine interview: "My music shows my feelings about life. I still have arthritis. But it doesn't have me."

It doesn't have me.

Max Cleland chose to go to Vietnam and he chose to throw himself on an enemy grenade. Byron Janis chose to experience the pain and agony of arthritis. But each man came to recognize that it was his choice, that he had the disease, the disease did not have him. Each chose to overcome those "limitations" and do more than most intact, healthy people ever dream of. We are not our bodies. Our bodies do not do it to us.

Sick Thinking

On Earth, it is our choice to get ill. We decide or cause or create colds and flus. We even have a cold and flu season. It's like going to spring training. One practices coming down with a cold. "I feel a cold coming on," we often hear. "I'm coming down with something." How many times have you heard people get into competition over how sick they are? "You think you gotta cold . . ."

Don't our beliefs and expectations frequently prove accurate? "The kids are back in school now, so the whole family is going to get sick soon with some bug they bring home. And once someone in our family gets sick, *everybody* in the family gets it. We like to share at our house." On Monday my brother-in-law will tell me he feels a little nasal congestion and a slight raspiness in his throat. He says that by Tuesday it will be settled in his chest, by Wednesday his nasal passages will be totally blocked, by Thursday he'll need at least half the day off, and by Friday the entire day off. He's predicting all this on Monday. Why do we do this to ourselves, Charlie Brown?

I'm not being flippant here. Even once-skeptical scientists and medical specialists have come to recognize a definite link between our psychological attitudes and the body's ability to ward off disease. The extent of those links, and how the links are forged, are not yet clearly understood. But the fact that such links exist is all but indisputable to the scientific community today.

The role of psychological factors in disease is demonstrated by the placebo effect. People who take what they think is a real drug, but is in truth an inert substance, often display the same *physiological* responses as if they had taken the real thing.

Scientific studies have reinforced that simple observation. In 1967 Thomas H. Holmes and R. H. Rahe published their "Social Readjustment Rating Scale." The scale ranks life experiences in the order of the amount of stress they typically cause in our lives. For instance, a person is most likely to suffer the greatest amount of stress following the death of a spouse. Ranked in descending order were divorce, marital separation, jail, and so on. The experiences included positive events (marriage, marital reconciliation, wanted pregnancies) as well as negative. Obviously, people react differently to the same event. Loss of a job can be devastating to some, an opportunity to others.

Scientific studies have shown that such stresses or depression can markedly affect the immunological system's ability to fight illnesses. One clinical study, for instance, showed that the level of disease-killing lymphocytes in the blood actually declined in healthy men whose wives had recently died of cancer. Another study showed that severe depression also weakens the body's immunological system. There is some evidence specific emotional traits trigger specific diseases: asthma may be a sign of a person feeling rejected, or a backache may mean a person wants to escape an intolerable situation. Illness is the body's way of coping with stress; there's nothing like a heart attack to slow one down or modify undesirable habits.

Laughter is the Best Medicine

If a strong link exists between our emotions and disease, we would expect evidence that a positive change in emotions and attitude can trigger improvement in our health. You probably don't need scientific studies to know that people with a bright, cheery outlook on life, people who have confidence in themselves, who respect themselves and others, typically are healthier than people who are always down in the dumps about something. Such studies do exist.

One recent study showed that patients who openly express their anger and determination to fight their cancers have a better chance of survival than those who suppress their feelings, who passively accept their condition. O. Carl and Stephanie Simonton, a husband-and-wife radiotherapist-psychologist team, described in their book, *Getting Well Again,* how imaging (the visualization of a desired result) plays a role in helping cancer patients combat their disease. Another study showed that asthmatic children who adjust well to their disease are less likely to die from an asthma attack than those who don't.

"Thanks doc. I'll let you know when I'm checking out."

For years, *Reader's Digest* has run a monthly section called "Laughter Is The Best Medicine." Norman Cousins, the former editor of *Saturday Review,* has written extensively on how laughter is just that. In his book, *Anatomy of an Illness,* Cousins described how through taking vitamin C, adopting a healthy mental attitude, and laughing a lot (he watched a lot of Marx Brothers movies) he cured himself of spinal arthritis.

The holistic ("whole-person") treatment of illness, which incorporates physical activity, daily relaxation, and psychological counseling, has gained wide acceptance in the medical community in recent years. An article in the British medical journal *The Lancet* concluded that "counseling in the acute phase of disease and psychological support in the chronic may be as important to outcome as many other therapeutic measures now undertaken."

It is also widely accepted that exercise, proper diet, and sufficient rest lead to a reduction in the frequency of illnesses or the shortening of the duration of illnesses. Are these not "choices" we make? Do we not choose to be healthy or not healthy? Even medicine's traditional physiological interventions in preventing and treating illness—immunization, public and private health measures, better surgical techniques, new ways to peer inside the body, and drugs—are merely the results of our "choosing" to conquer disease.

Of course, it is easier to blame invisible biological forces for our illnesses instead of taking responsibility for ourselves. An editor at the *New England Journal of Medicine* recently wrote in an editorial that if cancer in a person spreads, despite thinking positively, then is the patient at fault? At a time when patients are already suffering from the disease, wrote the editor, "they should not be further burdened by having to accept responsibility for the outcome." Which is precisely the point, of course. Accepting responsibility for one's outcome should never be a question . . . or a burden. People like Byron Janis and Max Cleland could not be living the dynamic lives they are if they had bought into this editor's dispirited view of life.

How far can the mind and spirit go in preventing the onset of disease, or combating it once it strikes? Once one recognizes that "I am" is in charge, not our bodies, what is there to stop us from eradicating disease entirely? Is immortality a reality? The claws of Death are being pushed back every day. The life span of cavemen averaged 19 years. Today the average life in the United States approaches 80. Individuals have lived 120 years or more. Is there a limit? Do we really believe there is a biological time line over which we cannot step? As I suggest in a latter chapter, "Limits of the Mind," our limits are self-imposed, that we in fact create our own reality. Disease and death are merely our own creation. We can "discreate" them as well.

*Belief systems are the concepts we use to run our lives. The problem with
a belief is that we take it to be the truth—and get stuck in it.*

—Adelaide Bry

8

A State of Mind

We are not our minds. Our minds do not do it to us.

As we do with our bodies, we allow our minds to control us.
We cling to the same beliefs we grew up with. We worry about
the future and feel guilty about the past. We are creatures of
habit. It's noon . . . must be time to eat. Hungry? . . . No, but
it's time to eat. Do you know people who go to bed the same
time every night, tired or not? Who sit in the same chair in the
same spot in the kitchen every meal? Who drive to work the
same route every day? Who believe they can't have pleasure all
the time? . . . pleasure one night a week, pain the other six.

Who is in charge here, anyway?

We cannot be home, in the present, making the choices we
want to make, if our minds are running us instead of the other
way around. Take a risk. Sit in a different kitchen chair for
dinner tonight. Sleep on the other side of the bed. It will mess
up the family, but everybody will be conscious for a change.

People not home are in one of three places: in the past, in the
future, or asleep.

Living in the Future

People who live in the future are either worriers or day-
dreamers. You can pick them out by the statements they make:

Some day I am going to be happy . . .
Only 15 years to retirement . . .

One of these days I'm going to take a vacation . . .
I can't wait until next week when . . .
I wish I could ski like they do . . .
I'm worried about . . .

A look at Present Moments

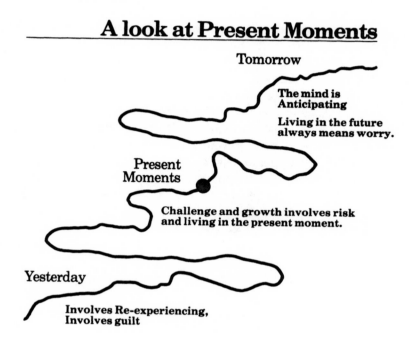

Tomorrow

**The mind is
Anticipating**

**Living in the future
always means worry.**

Present
Moments

**Challenge and growth involves risk
and living in the present moment.**

Yesterday

**Involves Re-experiencing,
Involves guilt**

My mother-in-law is a worrier. Her favorite TV channel is the Weather Channel. She doesn't realize that worrying or daydreaming about tomorrow causes her to completely miss today. I've never understood why some people worry *now* about tomorrow, and when tomorrow gets here they worry about it then, too, so they worry twice about the same thing. Remember worrying about your first date or your first honeymoon? No wonder most of them are disasters. We worry to death about them, and when they arrive we're such a wreck they turn into the disasters we worried they were going to be.

People worry about job interviews. They're certain they are

going to make a poor impression. They fret and chew their nails and don't sleep and fear the worst. And lo and behold, guess what happens? Any relationship there?

Of course, sometimes we fret about the future, yet when it arrives it's not half as bad as we feared, and we swear to ourselves we'll never worry again . . . and we don't, until the next time.

Worrying about the future is a waste of time because the future does not exist. The future is what you choose to create, and you cannot create it until you get there. The future is a now and nows can only be present moments.

Studies have revealed that the average person spends 40 percent of his or her waking hours daydreaming. But daydreaming also is a waste of time if you're not doing something *now* to accomplish what you're daydreaming about. My grandfather dreamed of opening a lawnmower repair shop. For the last 15 years of his working life at the Portsmouth, New Hampshire, Naval Shipyard he wished and wished about that repair shop. Finally he retired—and died two months later.

Living in the Past

Of course, many people drive down the road of Life trying to steer with their hands on the rearview mirror. You've heard their laments:

Back in the good old days . . .
I feel a lot of guilt about things I did earlier in my life . . .
When I was a boy . . .
We've always done it this way . . .
We can't make those changes . . .
Would you like to see a picture of me when I was on my high school football team . . .
I shoulda . . .
I coulda . . .

Like the future, the past does not exist. It never existed, because when what you think of as the past occurred it was a

94

now, and nows only can exist in the present. You can never change what has already occurred no matter how hard you strive because you can only make things happen in the present.

Semantics? A mind game? Nonsense? Yet like the people on Uranus, many of us try to live in the past. We try to change the past. Isn't that what guilt is all about—trying to change the past? Some of us were trained at Our Lady of Perpetual Guilt and Sorrow Forever. The teachers taught us to feel guilty, that guilt and fear are the road to personal growth. You've probably met a few of the top students, the ones who *wallow* in guilt, who are so covered in *chucas* (the guiltos) they can't function. Perhaps you've even met one or two of the really top students, the Mensa of guilt. They can feel guilty about the future, about events that have not even *happened* yet.

Like worrying, guilt is a wasted emotion. Feeling guilty about the past causes you to completely miss today. It is a condition of unconsciousness, which means it actually is a way to avoid taking responsibility for the present. I am willing to be held responsible for my past nows. Am I responsible for my divorce? Yes. One hundred percent. Do I feel guilty about it? Am I sorry for it? Nope. Why should I feel sorry for something I chose to do? I might apologize. Apologizing is acknowledging that I did not take total responsibility for something, which is certainly the case with my divorce. By negating guilt and sorry, and by accepting responsibility, I grow. I take that knowledge I learned from the experience that occurred yesterday (knowledge shoved aside by guilt) and apply it to the present, so I am more responsible for my current nows.

It is crucial each of us understands that our past nows do not determine our present nows—they only influence them.

My suggestion is that if you are a die-hard worrier or a guilt-ridden graduate of Our Lady of Perpetual Guilt and Sorrow Forever, you at least get organized about it. Between ten and eleven o'clock each evening do all your worrying and feeling guilty. Half an hour each. That way you can minimize the impact on the rest of your day.

A Silver Box

You can also spot people who live in the past because they often carry a little silver box under their arms. It's about the size of a music box and they store their special moments from the past in it—a special moment with a child, a relationship, a movie or a sports event, a lover, a dining experience. They carry this silver box with them all the time, and whenever they have a similar experience now they open the box to see if the now is as good as the one in the silver box. Nope, I guess it isn't. The service was much better the last time we were here. I better keep this one in here for another time.

Every time these people have a now, they compare it to past nows, instead of living in the now they're experiencing and doing what they can to make it a better now. They will hold up a present relationship to a past one, for instance, though it is comparing apples and oranges, instead of concentrating on making the present relationship work. They won't let go of their past, and consequently they miss the present.

Ladder of the Mind

Think of your mind as a ladder. The bottom rung is when you were born. Each subsequent rung represents a now in your life. One rung represents the time you slammed your fingers in the car door at age two. Another rung represents kick the can. Your first experience swimming. Your first girlfriend or boyfriend. Your first day at school. Your first kiss. The back seat of a '54 Ford. Your graduation from college. Military service. Your move to Chicago. Your first job. This rung is getting married. Moving into your first home. Your first child. Divorce. Starting your own business. All the way to the top rung, which represents this now right now. When you are on the top rung, when your body and mind and essence are all there at the same time, then you are conscious. When you slip below that line, you are *unc*.

One morning I was half an hour out of Denver on a flight to

96

Cleveland when the plane made an abrupt U-turn. I had been conscious up until then, when all of a sudden I chose to feel fearful. The guy next to me is nervously asking me what's happening just as I trigger back to when I last felt this scared.

I'm in boot camp and the tripod of the M-60 machine gun goes haywire and starts shooting the ground up all around us and I almost got hit which triggered me back to the time I got the car from dad and ended up drinking and driving and busting a headlight and having to tell dad which triggered when my sister died and I almost died which triggered when a friend hit me in the mouth with a rock which triggered . . . by then I finally climbed back to the top of the ladder and the guy next to me is still asking me what's going on and I'm saying, I don't know, I was just remembering when I got hit in the mouth with a rock, and the guy looks at me. . . .

Nothing is wrong with climbing back down those rungs now and then (as long as you're not flying the plane at the same time). Reliving memories at the high school reunion can be fun; living back in high school causes you to miss today. Checking memories can also serve as a useful guide for current choices. Triggering past nows of your parents teaching you to look both ways before crossing the street can keep you alive as you cross the street in your present now.

It is when we go below the line unconsciously or live there that we are missing out on life. When we let our past run us is when we wonder why we aren't enjoying our present nows. Some people call this living our old tapes or life scripts. "Parent tapes" are what most of us received from our parents, as a sort of bequeathment of memories. Parent tapes are recordings of the exact admonitions, inflections, screams, threats, and gestures they used to discipline and teach us when we were growing up. We internalize these tapes and store them away like 78 records in an old orange crate. When our children act in ways we consider inappropriate, or when we try to teach them something about life, we haul out the appropriate tape and plug it in and let it play.

When I was your age, son. . . .
Take your thumb out of your mouth or we'll be buying you
braces before you're ten years old . . .
I refuse to talk to a child who whines . . .
Don't ask me, ask your father . . .
No girl of mine dates before she's 18 . . .
You'll get warts doing that . . .
I can't believe you're two years old and you still can't go potty
by yourself . . .

We don't even think about whether the prerecorded message
we're broadcasting is appropriate, or even if what it says is something we really believe in. We just drop below that line into *unc*
and automatically punch in the tape—especially when the little
rug rats are screaming their heads off and painting on walls. Yet
we're shocked when our kids don't respond to us. They're experiencing and taking in and spitting out the language and the mores
and the rhythms of today while we're playing back to them tapes
originally recorded 20 and 30 years ago. Don't recycle those old
tapes. Record some new ones—your own tapes, tapes that truly
express your values of life and child rearing. Much of what your
parents taught you is probably worth keeping. Some of it isn't.
Discard what isn't valuable or timely, and keep the good stuff.
Incorporate what your experiences have taught you in recent
years.

Tapes are not exclusive to parent and child, of course. Marital
relationships, relationships with friends, or relationships at work
all build their own library of tapes. Have you ever watched a
marriage that's been together for a long time? Have you observed
how each person does and says exactly the same thing to each
other they've been saying and doing for the past 30 years? How
they goad each other, how one can turn off his or her internal
hearing aid when the other person is saying something they've
heard 1,345,299 times? It may be a marriage that's stayed together all these years (after all, they were taught that divorce is
a sin), but it is a marriage that is sleep walking. They both still
live in the same house but neither of them is home.

It's like each of us is a Wurlitzer. Remember the old record machine, with the bright rainbow on it and the panel of buttons and numbers and all those little records in a long row? Your favorite girl or favorite boy is with you and you push B17 and Connie Francis starts singing "Who's Sorry Now" and you hold hands and giggle a lot.

You walk up to the person and select a number on their personal Wurlitzer. If you know them, you know exactly which buttons to push. B17 . . . Looks like you're putting on a little weight, Ted. G39 . . . If you'd quit leaving your clothes all over the place our children would pick up theirs. P12 . . . Well, you just don't listen, do you. And if you don't know the person well, you just start randomly punching the buttons until you find one that works, until you play a song they can't stand.

Belief Systems

Attached to the ladder of the mind, like barnacles on the sides of a ship, are our belief systems. These are things we have come to believe or expect to be true. We learn them through personal experience or from what we learned from our family, friends, ministers, teachers, heroes, writers, society.

Common belief systems include:

Money is the root of all evil.
A woman's place is in the home.
Power corrupts, and absolute power corrupts absolutely.
A man's castle is his home.
Fat people are jolly . . . Thin are boring.
Stoves can be hot.
Children should be seen, not heard.
Black people are less intelligent than white people.
Irish people are drunks and fighters.
God is Christian, and a man . . . God is dead.
Look both ways before crossing the street.
All rape victims ask for it.
We should worry what others think of us.

Women can be emotional but not men.
Never die with holes in your underwear.

The Ladder of the Mind

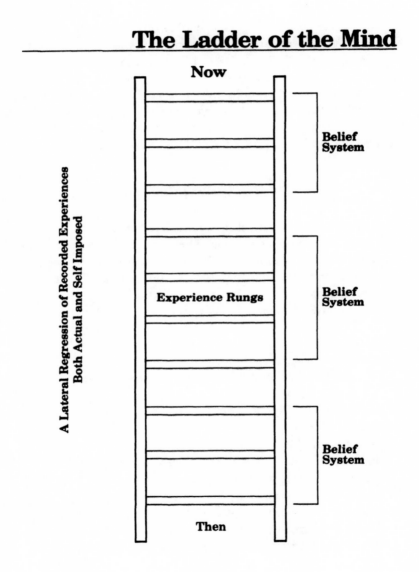

Now we can recycle these belief systems and let them run us, or we can consult them to see if they are still appropriate, and then use them or discard them as we experience our present nows. Yep, that one's good. Nope, that one's no longer valid.

That's not easy, of course. We cling to our belief systems because it is risky to cast them away, because they seem set in stone. Some of those set in stone in the past were:

The earth is flat.
The sun circles the earth.
Man was not meant to fly.
Unicorns exist.

At work your boss says you will be working on a project with Stephanie. Here's Stephanie . . . trigger, trigger, trigger . . . oh, oh, trouble. She wears a suit. Professional-looking . . . Belief system as taught by father and much of society is that a woman's place is in the home . . . Divorced, right? . . . Know how *she* got to where she is in the organization!

People who stay in the now, above the line, do not let out-dated belief systems run them. If a now triggers a past belief system, they evaluate it. Your experience working with women is that they have been just as competent as males. A woman's place in the home is no longer valid, you conclude. That was the way it was in the past. Now is different than then. Past nows should never determine how we act today. They are there as points for consultation, not dictation. And we can only evaluate those belief systems if we are conscious or aware that we have a choice. We must choose to make a difference!

Unc *Fighter*

When your mind runs you in an angry fashion, you have taken off in what I call the *Unc* Fighter. Remember Snoopy's Red Baron and his dog fights in the sky? Similar *unc* dogfights take place between husband and wife, co-workers, parents and children, brothers and sisters, or in any other relationship. When those *Unc* Fighters take off it means both people are below the line. They are unconscious. They have triggered the past and climbed back down the rungs of their ladders and stopped thinking about what they are doing. They may stop anywhere on the ladder—at a favorite belief system, an old and trusted memory, or all the way back to the rungs of their childhood. The intention of the *Unc* Fighter is to shoot the other person down, to make the other person wrong. Here's how it goes at my house.

"Dorothy, where's my billfold?"

"Probably where you left it."

Trigger, trigger, trigger . . . I make sure the bombs are fully loaded and the napalm ready; I climb into the cockpit of my *Unc* Fighter and turn it onto automatic pilot, take off, and climb to 35,000 feet.

"If this house was kept a little cleaner maybe I could find something when I look for it . . . rat-tat-tat." After a few moments I look down at the airfield and notice another *Unc* Fighter taking off. Moments later Dorothy comes in for the attack.

"I didn't notice your butt nailed to that chair . . . rat-tat-tat."

"Well, if I'm the one doing all the traveling and I have to do all the programs, the least you can do is take responsibility for . . . rat-tat-tat."

"I think you've mistaken me for someone who really gives a damn about your traveling and doing all the. . . ."

Two hours later, I'm yelling and she's crying and saying, "You never took me to nice places when we were dating," and I'm saying, "What the hell does that have to do with my lost billfold?"

To stop these dogfights and bring the *Unc* Fighters back to earth, one of you must get conscious about what is happening.

One of you must remember you are 100 percent responsible for your actions. One of you must choose not to play *Unc* Fighter. One of you must get home. "Excuse me, I think we are both *unc*. Let's take twenty minutes to cool down, get our thoughts together, and come back then to handle it." Take a walk and get conscious. Practice deep breathing. Be alone for a while, relax. Read a book. Needle point. Work in your stamp collection. Anything that will allow you mentally to take charge of your emotions.

It's Safe

We climb back down that ladder of the mind because it's safe down there, just as I did when the airplane I was on made the sudden U-turn. That's what makes old belief systems and old memories so appealing; they worked back then (though rarely as well as we remember them) so why change, why let go. Why challenge past nows with present nows whose results you're not sure about.

No wonder some people constantly dream about how much better tomorrow is going to be instead of facing the nows of today . . . it's safer, or at least they think it is. If you're living in poverty today, why not dream about tomorrow. Who wants to be home when home is full of rats and no food. Which is not to say anything is wrong with dreams or wishes. Dreams and wishes are the mists out of which solid goals are formed, and goals can lead to change. But if you live only tomorrow, in your dreams, you cannot be conscious in the present nows that will allow you to achieve those dreams. Remember, you can only make changes in the present now. You cannot make changes in a now that has already occurred or has yet to occur. Be conscious. If you're home more often you're less likely to let the mind run you. Think of the past as a positive place, full of fine memories, important thoughts, useful knowledge and experience. Choose to decide how much of that past information you're going to use. Learn from that past but don't live there. The same for the future. It is fine to think about the future, to anticipate, to set goals, to plan for tomorrow. But don't live there. Stay home.

This above all: to thine own self be true . . .
Thou canst not then be false to any man.
—William Shakespeare

9

Cleaning Out Our Tube

In his book, *The Book On The Taboo Against Knowing Who You Are,* Alan Watts wrote about the concept that each of us is a tube. We fill our tube during the day with food and water and we empty the tube in the bathroom. We fill our tube with experiences, and we empty many of them out of our tube through communication with other people. At the input end and the output end of our tube is a filter. We allow through the input filter the experiences and information we choose and we filter out the rest. At the output end we allow out through the filter the experiences and information we want to convey to others. So our tube and the other tubes we know are always giving and receiving communication through those filters; unfortunately, the filters frequently become clogged and require a thorough cleaning. What clogs our tube, in our personal and our professional lives, are things called lies.

Lying, to be truthful about it, is very popular in our culture. People routinely lie about their ages, grades, weight, income (It's estimated that $200 billion a year in income is under or unreported for income tax purposes), and why they are late to work (which is different from an excuse). Corporations lie about dumping toxic wastes. Harvard University medical researchers even lied about their data in research on an immune system stimulant. Presidents lie as a matter of policy. Eisenhower lied about the shooting down of Gary Powers, Kennedy lied about the invasion of Cuba, Johnson lied about the Gulf of Tonkin, Nixon lied about Watergate. Lying by advertisers is taken for granted. A car manufacturer even went so far as to do an expensive television "liars" campaign built on the theme that what you hear in many TV ads are lies, or at the least, exaggerations. It's no surprise that polls show that 60 percent of us feel it's okay to lie sometimes, particularly to protect someone else's feelings.

But lying is merely one more way we hamper ourselves from living fully in the present moment, from being alive and alert and anticipatory and energized and making the choices we desire instead of being stuck with experiences we could have done without. When you have had a lie running between you and someone else, how do you feel in your gut? . . . Anxious? . . . Guilty? . . . Insecure? And we know now that when we feel anxious or guilty we aren't living in the present. When we deal with that person we're thinking about the past or the future— we're not home. We keep trying to push that lie away and it just keeps coming back. So if you want to be 100 percent *effectively* responsible for your life, you have to come from the truth all of the time.

People lie, of course, for the same reason they live in the past or the future: they don't want to be responsible for themselves. If I lie to myself about why I'm overweight then I don't have to face the fact I am responsible for my being overweight, not someone or something else. If I have to acknowledge my responsibility, that might mean I'm going to have to do something about it because why on earth would I want to *choose* to be overweight (unless I want to be a Sumo wrestler).

Lies of Omission

Two kinds of lies clog the filters of our tubes. One is a lie of omission. That's when the person we are lying to is ourself. Also known as kidding ourself. My number one lie of omission for many years was my being overweight, which I blamed on those people in China, my mother, my big bones. My tube was stuck about that. I needed to clean out my tube, to tell myself the truth.

People used to say, "Hey, Ted, looks like you're losing weight."

"Yeah. I'm trying."

Now when they ask, I say, "No, I'm not losing weight. But thanks for checking. I appreciate your interest."

You've been telling people forever at cocktail parties you are going back to school to get that degree. You know that is crap. Inside, you know you have no intention whatsoever of going back. Clean out your tube.

Then there's the biggest lie of all we tell ourselves: I'm going to quit smoking.

As I discussed in the section of Belief Systems, each of us has our ways of thinking and processing designed or wired in a specific way, so that each time we face a specific now with decisions that need to be made we handle them the way we have been taught or designed to think. I came out of a divorce after ten years of marriage looking for love in my life. I'm talking here about love, not sex—about the caring, feeling, emotional sharing and development with another person. I had certain belief systems that taught me the way and who I was supposed to love. I had been taught that a man couldn't find love from other men, for instance. That ruled out 50 percent of the population. At the same time, I couldn't love all women because they could only fall between the ages of 22 and 45, and within that age bracket they had to be physically attractive, with big bazooms, of similar socioeconomic background (preferably with money), personal development, and on and on. I had it wired up to this tiny segment of the population, and on top of that they had to love me first. No wonder I couldn't find love. I was lying to myself. I had to clean that portion of my tube out, I had to tell myself the truth that I had to love myself before I could love anyone else, and what I gave to myself was what I was going to give to someone else. That allowed me to have the freedom and the growth to be able to have love from people from all parts of the population, men and women. That allowed me to love an 87-year-old man and a 2-year-old girl. That allowed me to realize that what I was able to put out, I was able to get back.

I find that when I tell the truth more in my interactions with people, personally and professionally, that I have much more effective relations coming back also.

Clean out the tube. It's easier to live fully if we admit to ourselves, "Hey, I don't plan to quit right now." Remember, there is no such thing as trying. You either do or you don't do. Worrying about trying only fouls up the nows.

Lies of Commission

Lies of commission are the lies we tell others. Often these are the same lies we tell ourselves, but sometimes they are lies we spin to protect ourselves from others or even to protect them from some "truth" we think they should not know "for their own good" or that we feel "they cannot handle."

Tubeness

Experience
Intention
Truth

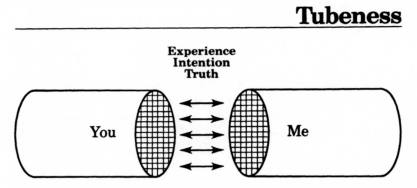

Late on a Friday afternoon someone asks you to mail their utility bill. They have a disconnect notice. "Sure, I'll be glad to," you say. Monday morning you're at the dry cleaners emptying the suit pockets and . . . oh, shit. You run down to the utility company, pay the bill, and go to the office. You're scared. All day you avoid the person. You screwed up and you're afraid to acknowledge it. Your tube is clogged. You're ineffective at work; your mind is on that damn utility bill. How do you feel inside? You know the only way to correct it, to unclog that tube.

"I forgot to mail the bill for you Friday. I acknowledge that I failed to take total responsibility to see that it got done. If they charge you for turning your power back on I'll pay for it."

Truth is the only thing that works all the time. Lying,

whether it is conscious or unconscious lying, is one more way we attempt to deny our total responsibility for ourselves. We are trying to disown our feelings and behavior when we lie to ourselves or to others.

You're out of town at a seminar. Your spouse remains at home. It's an interesting seminar, you meet an interesting person, you go with them for a little attitude adjustment afterwards which turns into dinner and drinks, and ultimately a little extracurricular activity.

You return home, full of guilt. The *chucas* are crawling all over you. Your tube is clogged. You create diversions the next few weeks by perpetrating conflicts about the kids, work, the house, which movie to see—anything to avoid the real issue gnawing at you. You're probably not conscious when you make love. Your nows are disasters because of your lie.

A woman once asked me during a seminar, "Ted, you've been telling us to live in the now. So why do I have to tell my husband about the then?"

Good question, and my answer is that to the extent yesterday is affecting you today, you have to tell the truth.

Do You Want the Truth?

Do you want the truth all the time? Or do you prefer people lie to you whenever *they* think it is appropriate and timely? Do you want them to filter information to you, or would you rather hear the truth so you can decide for yourself how to react to the information?

Much has been written the last few years about how our own presidents have been lied to by their intelligence agencies and their advisors; they've been told what they want to hear and not what really happened. Who among the president's friends and appointees want to tell the president his or her foreign policy has a problem? Many of us seem to want to live in the same dream world—don't bother me with the truth. I don't want to know I'm dying of cancer or my kid is on drugs or my spouse is having an affair. Yet we always know anyway, don't we, and it gnaws at us. We may not know the details, but we know something is wrong. And deep down inside we're angry that the people around us are lying to us. So why should we lie so easily to them?

You have a report due on your boss's desk at 4 p.m. Friday. Your boss leaves at 2 p.m. for the day. Saved. The report you didn't have ready can now be finished over the weekend. Drop it on the boss's desk at 7 a.m. and the boss will never know. But you will. One more piece of crud in your tube's filter.

If you can lie to your boss, is it all right that your boss lies to you? "The company's never been on better financial footing," says your boss. The next day the company declares bankruptcy. "You're doing a terrific job here." The next day you arrive to find your desk in the street, set afire. What's your likely reactions to these situations? Anger, sure. Yet if you've lied to your boss how can you expect more back than you have been willing to give?

Companies and governments lie to their people all the time, of course. Governments typically justify it by cloaking it under "national security." Companies either make no excuses or attribute it to "competitive reasons." Regardless, there is no excuse to lie. What is permissible, to me, is for a company or government official to say, "That's confidential. I am not at liberty to comment." That means, I know the truth but I cannot or will not release that information at this particular moment. But that sort of thing really should be rare (far rarer than it is). What is far more common is simple bold-faced lying for no reason other than to cover one's rear.

Now how did our top government and company officials learn to lie? From many sources, probably, but most likely the primary source was their parents. Parents often lie to their kids—"We'll go to the zoo *next* week," they say, just to get the kid off their back and with absolutely no intention of going. Or their kids overhear them lying to someone else.

An acquaintance calls to invite you to dinner. "Gee, we'd love to come," you say, "but we've got other plans."

"What plans?" your daughter asks after you hang up.

"Oh, we'll think of something."

I was at the grocery store one day with my son, Scott. I'm in the checkout line and the clerk is going over my check ... Is this your current address and phone number? ... I'm *unc* and I reply, yes. Scott looks at me and says, "No, dad, we just moved, remember?" I'm thinking, I got six people waiting behind me, and I know there's money in the account and I just haven't had time to order new checks, so it's okay if I just pretend nothing's changed. But it's not. It's never okay to lie. So I take out a new check and write in the new information. Outside I thank my son for getting me conscious. "That's okay, dad." Don't you love kids!

Little White Lies

People frequently ask me about white lies ... People frequently ask me to tell white lies.

"What do you think of my new dress, Ted?"

I think you should use it to wrap dead fish in. But of course, I say, "It's lovely."

Wouldn't it be better to say, "I prefer you in blue" or "I really don't care for that color on you" or "I don't believe that dress compliments you the way you desire."

Or more commonly, at work you pass someone in the hallway who says, "Hi, how are you? How about lunch? Give me a call." Sure, sure, you're nodding to all this, with absolutely no intention of going to lunch with the person.

Typically what I say when someone asks me for an opinion— and as you might guess, not many do anymore—is, "Do you want me to tell you what you want to hear or what I really feel?"

How to tell the truth is something I will discuss later in the chapter on leveling. Suffice it at this point to be aware that you can tell the truth responsibly or irresponsibly. It is the difference between leveling and dumping. Dumping is the irresponsible communication of the truth. It's replying, "That dress stinks." Leveling is the responsible communication of the truth. It's saying, "No thanks, I appreciate the invitation to lunch but I prefer not to," or "Yes, it has been a while since we've seen each other. How are the kids?"

As for the issue of who decides what is the truth, that is simple. You do. Truth isn't an absolute. Truth is your reality, your perception of reality, and only you know what your reality is. You'll know when you're lying to yourself, and most people will know it too.

10

The Limits of the Mind

Let's begin with a familiar exercise. Below are nine dots set in rows of threes. Study them for a few moments. You probably see one large square and four small squares out of that set of nine dots. Perhaps you see an X. What else? Triangles, a cross, rectangles? From those nine dots you can make every letter in the alphabet, as do a dot matrix printer or an electronic scoreboard. The dots may remind you of things you've seen in your past nows . . . Tic Tac Toe . . . Hollywood Squares . . . playing chess . . . dice . . . four square . . . a dress you owned once . . . a pattern in a tie . . . a screen on a computer terminal . . . a cribbage board . . . peg board in your garage . . . circle irrigation from 37,000 feet.

Now take a pencil and interconnect all nine dots using four straight lines, without lifting your pencil off the paper from the moment you begin to draw until you are finished. Reread that carefully. Be Here Now. Take your eye off the television. Connect all nine dots using four straight lines *without lifting your pencil.* Please do not do what you think I asked you to do. Do only what I am asking.

•   •   •

•   •   •

•   •   •

Before you read further, turn to the end of this chapter to see one method for completing that exercise.

Did you only try to draw those four lines *within* the confines of the square? I never instructed you to stay within the square; yet most people who attempt this exercise for the first time *assume* they are to stay within the square. Most people *assume* the square to be the limitations of their reality. The human spirit tends to confine its reality to a very tight, proscribed box. Remember growing up and being applauded by your parents when you learned to color *inside* the lines with your crayons? Never assume anything. It makes an *ass* out of *u* and *me*.

John C. Lilly, M.D., is a neurophysiologist who has studied dolphins for over 20 years, trying to learn the capacity of their intelligence and to communicate with them. His work, pioneering and controversial, has earned him the title of the father of modern dolphin research. Lilly wrote the following in his book, *The Center of the Cyclone:*

> In the province of the mind, what one believes to be true either is true or becomes true within certain limits to be found experientially and experimentally. These limits are further beliefs to be transcended. In the province of the mind, there are no limits.

In the province of the mind, there are no limits.

Whatever you think, whatever you believe to be true, is true for you. I remember when I was growing up having childhood discussions with a friend about "accepting reality." He believed that the best course in life was to accept reality. Who was going to define reality was arguable, of course, but my friend believed there were certain realities that everyone agreed on and that were inviolable. War was a reality. Death was a reality. Money was a reality. To argue otherwise was foolish and foolhardy. You prepared for reality like you prepared for an exam: you studied, you marked the correct answers, and if you were smart enough or you cribbed the answers stealthily enough, you passed reality— meaning you didn't die in combat, you made money, and you stayed out of the funny farm.

114

Most of us live our lives "accepting reality." Most of us spend a lot of our day listening to other people—or ourselves—tell us what we can and cannot do. We don't do it that way here . . . That's a fact of life, son . . . That won't work . . . You can't . . . Face the facts . . .

"Can't" Means "Won't"

"I just can't remember people's names, you know. I got this thing about names." When I hear that I usually ask them how big their thing is.

What people are really saying is they have accepted that as their reality and they won't change it. "Can't" always means "won't." At some of my seminars I assign each participant the task of learning the names of every other participant (usually 20 to 25 names) by the end of the three days. On the last day I ask some individuals to stand up and name every person in the room. For many participants, that is a large challenge. But they nearly all succeed because they took the responsibility to be aware and learn the other participants' names, even if failing to remember names is a typical "reality" for them.

"I can't speak in front of large groups. I don't speak up and I'm very shy. I lack confidence in myself."

"I'm a very confident person. I'm outgoing, an extrovert. I feel comfortable talking before groups."

Each of these statements are reflections of the speakers' beliefs about themselves. If people see themselves as shy, then they will prove to themselves and others that they are. They accept reality, in which reality becomes a self-fulfilling prophecy. Pianist Byron Janis realized that reality was not that arthritis prevented him from playing beautiful music; arthritis was merely a "limitation" that had to be overcome.

Running is very popular these days. How far, in the province of your mind, can you run? Half a mile? One mile? By experimenting and experiencing, that is the limit you have found. At the end of one mile you feel like buying the franchises on bottled oxygen and crutches. Yet the limit in your mind can be transcended. Each day you run you shoot for a few more yards, another quarter mile. Before you realize it, you are running two, three, five miles. You keep transcending your previous limits. You may eventually become a marathoner, despite the fact that when you started out you said, "No way can I run 26 miles."

How many athletes do you think "accepted reality" when they first heard about triathlons? "Me, run 26 miles 385 yards, bike 112 miles, and swim another 2 1/2 miles, all in 10 hours? You must be nuts!"

When they held the first triathlon in Hawaii only a handful of people showed up. Today thousands participate, including men and women in their sixties and diabetics who take insulin during the competition. Limits of the mind? What limits?

At one time reality said there were eight planets that circled the sun, not nine. But we've since transcended that reality. Was there ever the reality that man could not fly? People could always fly. They simply never believed it.

> I can't have my own business.
> I'll never get promoted.
> I'll never sell my novel.
> I'll never make the team.
> I'll never find the woman of my dreams.
> I can't climb that cliff.

You don't "can't." You choose not to. You create your own reality.

Pygmalion

In 1964 in Oakland, California, in an experiment called "Pygmalion in the Classroom," 120 eighth-grade students were administered the Stanford Benet Intelligent Quotient test, also commonly known as an IQ test. The norm is around 100. Above average is 110–120, superior is 120–135, and above that is gifted. Below 80 falls slow learners and the significantly limited.

After the students were tested, the school administration ran-

116

domly placed the kids in five 9th-grade classes. Each student and each student's teacher were informed of the results of the IQ test. Unbeknownst to the teachers and the students, however, was that only half the IQ scores were legitimate. The other half were in fact the students' locker numbers. At the end of the first grading period the students with the legitimately higher IQ's had the higher grades. The kids with the legitimately lower IQ's received the lower grades. Correspondingly, the students with the higher locker numbers received higher grades, and the students with the lower locker numbers received lower grades.

In the province of the mind, what one believes to be true either is true or becomes true . . .

Without getting into the issue of the validity of IQ tests, it is evident that the experiment in Oakland and many similar studies illustrate how "labeling" someone—which is done all the time in our schools and society—can adversely alter how the individual and people around the individual perceive and act toward that person. If we label a child as "retarded" we have destroyed that child. As an encyclopedia noted about such IQ tests, "Since an individual's IQ does not usually vary greatly from year to year, it affords a basis for predicting his probable future achievement; its value for school placement is therefore apparent."

When we use tests or labels to "predict" someone's future, when that individual, as well as the people around the individual, believe that prediction, it will become true. When we operate from effect instead of cause we allow outside events and people to dictate how we will respond and act. "My IQ test says I'm a moron. I must be if it says I am."

Past experiences or other beliefs about ourselves do not determine our future; they only influence it. How much we let it influence us is the question. If you live life from effect instead of cause, if you do not believe yourself responsible for yourself, I wish you a high locker number in life.

For fun, let's do an experiment that demonstrates how easily one can transcend the limits of one's mind. You need a friend for this, preferably one of your approximate size and strength. Face your friend and extend your strongest arm straight out, palm up and elbow pointed toward the floor, and make a fist. Have your friend grasp your wrist in one hand and the back of your upper arm in the other, and attempt to bend your arm back (in its natural direction) until your fist touches your shoulder while you resist with all your strength. Unless you are exceptionally strong or your friend exceptionally weak, your friend will be able to bend your arm back. Exchange roles with your friend and repeat the exercise.

Now repeat the experiment, only this time I want you to imagine that a steel rod is running up through your body, through your arm and fist, and out into infinity. Once that image is secure in your mind, nod to your friend to again try to bend your arm. Keep that image in your mind! Feel that steel rod in your body, see it shooting out of your fist into space. Now there is a good chance your friend cannot bend that arm back at all, or if he or she is able to, it is with far greater difficulty than before. You have transcended the previous limits you thought existed for the strength of your arm, without any change except in your mind. What other limits have you enclosed yourself with? What other limits have you established that are waiting to be broken?

Creating a New Reality

Each of us is constantly creating a new reality. Each now is a new reality. The only thing that is limiting that reality is our failure to ask ourselves new questions. We cannot grow if we continue to ask the same old questions. We keep creating the new nows like we created the old ones, plugging along on the same road, never looking to see if there are new directions we can explore, new roads to travel.

Remember my description of my arrival at the airport in Denver right after a record-breaking Christmas snow storm? I'm standing there by the luggage carousels, ranting and raving about the piles of passengers and the lack of taxicabs and the drifts of snow and why wasn't the mayor getting the roads plowed and where the hell was my tax money going to when my daughter Megan interrupted my diatribe. "Dad," she said, "do you want to get home?" Why do daughters ask their fathers such inane questions at times like that? "Come with me then," she said. We rounded up a skycap, loaded the bags, and went back into the terminal, up the escalator, and out to the entrance where cabs were dropping people *off*.

When we fail to be creative, we fail to think outside the square box, we fail to break those limits of our mind, we fail to transcend reality because we prefer to spend our energy shirking responsibility and finding fault with others. While I'm standing there trying to make other people wrong for what I was experiencing, my daughter was asking herself, where else can we get a cab?

The notion of creating one's own reality may sound like the sort of metaphysical hot-tub gobbledygook that came out of California in the 1960's. Yet there is increasing scientific evidence that we indeed create the physical reality we see around us. This falls into the branch of physics known as quantum mechanics, which studies the behavior of subatomic particles. One experiment, known as the delayed-choice experiment, suggests that the scientific observer may actually be able to determine which path a randomly projected subatomic particle takes before it reaches its target. As one physicist said at a recent conference, "The experimental evidence suggests that we have a role in creating the universe."

Physicists are far from unified on this notion, but they are asking new questions that may someday prove from a scientific standpoint a question that philosophy has wrestled with for eons.

Expectations

What is reality but expectations? We assume or expect certain things to happen, and lo and behold they do most of the time. Indeed, we have reached the point where we *expect* to be done to and we learn to "cope" with those expectations. What are our expectations about doctors and dentists—if our appointment with them is at 3:00 p.m., we won't get in to see them until

4:00 p.m. ("The doctor had an emergency today.") Those magazine articles that tell us how to "cope" with life give us tips on how to keep from becoming stressed about the situation ("Go prepared: take a good book or your knitting. Remain calm."). We accept the ignominy of the situation as though it was a penalty in the game called Life, an unlucky roll of the dice. Yet, why should we allow the doctor to do that to us? Do his or her framed diplomas and steep office charges entitle the doctor to treat us that way?

What many of us fail to realize is we created this reality in the first place, and if we choose to we can create a different reality. In the case of doctors and dentists, I chose to change my reality. I interviewed by telephone several doctors and dentists. I told each doctor that I knew they expected to be paid promptly for services rendered and that they did not expect me to be late to my appointment or to cancel at the last minute. I explained to them that I expected the same commitment from them. I offered each doctor the following arrangement: if I canceled less than 24 hours prior to my scheduled appointment I owed them the cost of an office visit. In turn, if they did not see me on time they owed me the price of an office call, which they could stick on the other side of the ledger for the next time. I called twelve doctors and seven dentists before I found two who would agree to my proposal. Guess who gets seen on time?

I and several partners built the $13.5 million office building in which I have my offices. What are the typical expectations today for constructing a building or a power plant or a highway or a jet fighter? . . . It won't be finished on time and it will cost more than originally projected. The government and corporations *plan* for cost overruns. Why do we do this to ourselves? Why do we accept this as reality?

When my partners and I decided to build this building we asked for bids. We held a meeting one day which 32 contractors attended. We wanted to know for how much they would put up the building and when they would finish it. Each gave us their figures. We then told them that the contract would stipulate that if the building was not completed on time and within budget, the contractor would *pay us* $150,000 each day beyond

120

the deadline. Thirty of the 32 contractors left the room. Two stayed. We picked one. The building was finished 30 days ahead of schedule and within budget. We recognized we had choices. We recognized we could create our own reality. We expected the contract to be fulfilled on time, and we saw to it that our expectation was met.

Another "reality." It is fashionable to be late these days. Dinner parties begin at 7:00, but nobody shows up until 7:30, with the stragglers showing up at 8:00 or after. It is as though it were unseemly to arrive anywhere *on time*. We expect people to be late.

I have a friend who was always late for dinner. I'd ask him over and he'd say, fine, what time?, and I'd say seven and he'd say, fine ... and he'd be late every time. Naturally he had excuses, usually that his wife was late putting on her makeup. He was making her responsible for him not being there on time. My wife and I were experiencing the result of their being late, too. In our place, most people would blame my friend for the fact that they were not able to serve dinner on time. It was his fault because he and his wife were late. After a while it becomes a matter of expectations. Bob and Martha are coming for dinner Saturday, dear. I told them seven, so let's plan on serving dinner at eight.

But in my world, I don't accept those expectations, or realities, that I don't want. I choose to create new realities. In the case of Bob, I invited him to dinner one day and he said fine and I said, "Oh, by the way Bob, we're having barbecued steaks. Really thick juicy ones. I'm putting the steaks on the grill at seven. You're responsible for turning yours over." Guess what time Bob and his wife arrived?

Other Expectations

We all deal with vendors in one way or another: furnace cleaners, plumbers, auto mechanics, real estate brokers, public relations firms, house cleaners, appliance repair persons, restaurants, insurance salespersons, ad infinitum. What are your expectations when you deal with them? I'm not asking what are your hopes.

I know what your hopes are: they do the job correctly, on time, and for the price they quoted. But what do you expect? The worst, of course. They'll promise you the moon to get a sale and deliver you moonbeams. So why don't you create a reality in which your expectations match your hopes?

I wanted $5,000 worth of manuals for my seminars. The salesman gave me his standard sales pitch and I said fine, I'll make a deal with you if you can have them delivered by October 1 . . . Sure, sure, no problem . . . I need them here by October 1, no later . . . no problem, he reassured me . . . I could tell he was not coming from the same sense of responsibility I was. I told him subtly that it was really important to me that he said what he was going to do and that he did what he said he would. I will be glad to make a contract with you if the manuals will be here by October 1 . . . No problem, he reassured me again. The company was in Des Moines, but he did not expect any problem in shippage . . . But you see, I told him, I don't care if there is a problem in shippage. I don't care if you have to drive to Des Moines yourself to pick them up. I want them here by October 1. Do we still have a deal? . . . Sure . . . I was still sensing that this man was not completely conscious, so I said, for every day that the manuals are overdue I am going to deduct $2,000 from my bill. Do you still want my business? That got him conscious. He excused himself, borrowed my telephone, returned in twenty minutes, and said, yes, he would make the commitment.

The manuals arrived September 15.

The only person who suffers the consequences when your supplies are not delivered on time or your car is not fixed properly or the meal arrives cold and undercooked is guess who? Do you realize how many people out there are hungry for your business? Yet most of us mumble through, bitch and moan when things go wrong, and then accept the indignities on top of that. Why? Because we expect—and consequently receive and accept—inferior service and shlock work. We accept the conventional reality that many people in this country do a half-assed job at whatever job they work.

You go to the grocery store. You expect to stand in line, often a long line. Why do you do that to yourself? I don't. I walk up to the manager and say, excuse me, would you mind checking me out of here. I'm in a hurry. Almost always they get somebody for me. If they don't, I guess I chose to wait that day.

Parking is another favorite of mine. Our expectation is that a parking place is always tough to find. My expectation is that I will always have my parking place where I want it to be. Recently I was in southern California with my daughter, and we were staying with a friend in Newport Beach. I wanted to take Megan to Century Plaza in Los Angeles to see the play *Evita*, so I asked my friend John if he could get us some reservations for Friday or Saturday night.

The first thing out of his mouth was, "We can't."

Why? I asked

"There's no place to park."

What? This was five days before we would be there, and he had already decided that we would not have a parking place when we got there. So I told him to get us the tickets and that I would get us a place to park. I said I would drive his car because he obviously had no place to park, but that I . . . have a place to park.

"What are you talking about?" he asked.

Because I always have my place. I always expect to have my parking place up front and I always choose to have it. I don't want to go with someone who has already decided he doesn't have a place.

So John made reservations for us, and on Friday night we drove up from Newport Beach with my friend in the back seat and Megan and I up front. We were driving along the freeway in heavy traffic and my friend was laughing I-told-you-so because the traffic was bumper to bumper.

Relax, John, I said, I don't have a place here on the freeway. My place is downtown. If I had wanted a place on the freeway I'd have one, but I don't need one here now. We finally got off the freeway and down to Century Plaza, and I didn't see my place.

"Where's my place, Megan?"

"Somebody must be using it," she said.

We drove around the block and spotted a little lady coming

out of a lot right off an alley near the theater. As she pulled away, I yelled to her, "You're welcome. I hope you enjoyed my place."

You see, I don't mind someone using my parking place if I'm not there, but it is my place. I always have my place right up front, because it is just as easy to expect to have a parking place up front as it is in the back. My friend in Newport Beach, of course, believes life is a flat bitch . . . and then you get to die.

Ask new questions. Accept no reality except the realities you want. Otherwise, who is the only person who ends up sucking pond water with a straw?

Creativity

Refusing to accept old realities, old nows, old limitations, is at the root of creativity. I'm not going to attempt to detail the many tricks and techniques people use to be creative. Entire books, some of them very good, have been written about the subject. The important point is these tricks and techniques are useless if you are not a person who is in charge of yourself in the first place. Creativity springs from control, self-confidence, and intuition.

Webster's dictionary defines "create" as "to cause or occasion." It is difficult to cause something if you play from effect, have old expectations, cling to old belief systems, aren't home, let your mind and body run you. Many people lack creativity and imagination because they spend their energy trying to make others wrong. These people make up the majority of the world. They are the critics. They are the ones who limit their horizons, fail to produce, accept mediocrity, and find life dull and uneventful. They exist their life away.

Tom Peters, co-author of the book *In Search of Excellence,* was speaking at a Young Presidents Organization seminar when one of the participants stood up and angrily said to Peters, "You've been berating us for nearly two days about how average we are, how we're not reaching for quality. I'm sick of it. We're no worse than anybody else." To which Peters replied, "Great. Can we put that on your letterhead?"

The creative souls, the ones who only use their belief systems and memories and past nows as sources of reference and information, who recognize they are responsible for themselves and their actions, are the doers. They are the ones who rise high on the corporate ladder or who stake out a new and profitable business, who write great books and paint great pictures, who contribute significantly to humankind, who make life fun and adventurous.

Creativity is action. When it comes to problems, for instance, creativity is the difference between focusing on the problem and focusing on the solution. Critics focus on the problem: you shoulda . . . you coulda . . . if you had done this . . . They are looking for a person or thing on which to fix blame. They spend endless hours examining how and why it happened, making the problem larger than it was in the first place. They recycle those belief systems and old tapes.

Critics remain mystified by creativity. They see it as something mythical, something the Muses pass down to a chosen few (reinforcing their belief that outside forces determine each person's reality).

Doers know better. They recognize that creativity and imagination are consequences they cause to happen. Doers focus on the solution to a problem. They examine how to do things differently the next time. They communicate with others instead of seeking to pin blame on others. They focus on strengths instead of weaknesses. They redefine the problem as a goal. Instead of "I am lonely," a doer says "I want friends." Instead of "How do I stop arguing with my kids?" a doer says "I want to get along better with my kids." It is the difference between the positive and the negative.

I have a neighbor who has been trying to sell his home for two years. He has many expectations and many excuses: the housing market is flat, the interest rates are too high, too many people are out of work, his house falls in the wrong price bracket, the house up the street is unpainted. His lament is not unique. A lot of critics have houses on the market.

Not so the doers. The doers recognize they and they alone are responsible for selling their house, and so they use their imagination and creativity to make certain the house sells. Take

Stanleigh Fox of suburban Chicago. Fox and his roommate wanted to sell their $143,000 house. Besides the usual hurdles of a slow market and high interest rates, it was dead winter in Chicago, the most difficult time to sell a home. A four-day ad in a local newspaper had brought a meager four phone calls. But Fox and his roommate refused to accept that as reality. Instead, they chose to ask new questions, to take action. What imaginative approach would intrigue the snow-bound Chicago home buyer?

The result was a sign posted in their front yard that said:

HOUSE FOR SALE

BY OWNER

FREE HAWAIIAN VACATION

FOR TWO

By the end of the first day they had received 30 inquiries. The Associated Press wrote a story about the gimmick. It did not take long for Stanleigh Fox and his roommate to sell their home.

I sensed the same positive action-approach in an article I read in which several senior planners at the Raytheon Corporation speculated about the home of the future. One remark that struck me was the statement that "A washing machine is not necessarily a device that washes by wetting. It's a machine to separate fabric from dirt, and perhaps that doesn't require water at all." That's the kind of imaginative thinking that produces new and useful products. It comes from someone not content with recycling old ways, from someone who asks new questions.

The Steel Pipe

Let's conduct another exercise, similar to the dot exercise, to stretch the limits of the mind. Below is an illustration of a steel pipe embedded in the concrete floor of a bare room. The inside

126

diameter of the pipe is .06" larger than the diameter of a ping-pong ball (1.50") that is resting gently at the bottom of the pipe. You and five other people are in the room along with the following objects:

100' of clothesline
A carpenter's hammer
A chisel
A box of Wheaties
A file
A wire coat hanger
A monkey wrench
A light bulb

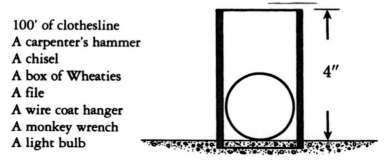

4"

Take five minutes to think of as many ways as possible to get the ball out of the pipe without damaging the ball, the pipe, or the floor. When the five minutes are up, look at the end of this chapter at some suggested solutions.

Did you focus on the problem instead of the solutions? Did you have trouble shaking off your old belief systems? Did the idea of floating the ball out by urinating in the pipe fail to surface because your belief system told you to never do something like that in mixed company, or because it sounded repulsive? Did you think of the resources in their conventional sense and fail to look at them in different ways?

Creativity comes when we get out of our own way. It comes when we shed our past nows and concentrate on the now at hand. To take total personal responsibility for ourselves requires creativity and imagination, just as the roots of creativity and imagination lie in accepting responsibility for ourselves. Most of us believe that traffic makes us late to work. Creative thinking understands that traffic has nothing to do with it. Traffic does not care. Creative thinking says, I was late because I failed to allow myself enough time to get to work on time. Creativity and imagination are a matter of attitude, a matter of expectations, a matter of asking new questions, of drawing outside the lines, of playing from cause instead of effect, of creating new realities, of transcending the previous limits of the mind.

Expanding the limits of our minds is vital in a world in danger of blowing itself to bits or choking to death in its own wastes and excesses. It is vital to our livelihoods as our economy becomes more global and interdependent with other economies, as we shift from an industrial society to an information society. It is vital to our personal well being as we struggle to adapt to a world that seems to spin faster and faster each day.

*DOT EXERCISE

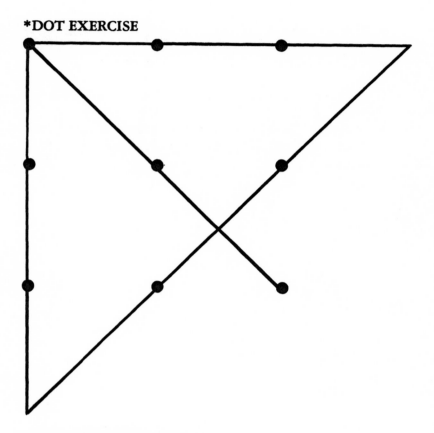

*STEEL PIPE EXERCISE
(suggested answers)

- Take the hammer, flatten the coat hanger, wedge it under, and lift up the ball.

- Flatten both ends of the hanger and make tweezers out of it.

- Moisten the glue top on the Wheaties box and stick it to the ball.

- Crush the Wheaties and stuff them down the side of the ball to displace it.

- Suck the ball up.

- Urinate in the pipe to float the ball to the top.

- Roll up the wax paper in the Wheaties box and suck it up.

- Take the light bulb, rub it against your clothing to create static electricity, and put the tip of it against the ball to pull out.

If any man thinketh that he is wise among you in this world, let him become a fool, that he may become wise.

—*St. Paul*

11

The Truth Seeker

Once upon a time there was a truth seeker. This truth seeker was looking for meaning in her life. She wanted to know what is the real way life should work, so she could hang everything she had learned on it and make everything work. She threw herself into religious organizations, cults, communes, rolfing, meditation, yoga, California hot tub groups, the Grateful Dead—anything that claimed to hold the secret to life's eternal truths. She played tapes of rock albums backwards, listening for Satanic messages. She took college courses in Oriental and Greek philosophy, stayed up late in dormitories discussing such weighty issues as does a tree that falls in the forest make a noise when no one is around to hear it?

She read all the source documents she could lay her hands on: the *Bible*, the *Koran*, the *Bagavad Gita*, the *Torah*, the *Book of Mormon, Zen and the Art of Motorcycle Maintenance*, the *Book of the Hopi*. She studied the latest books on the latest discoveries in physics. She spent 15 years and thousands of dollars in this relentless search. Finally, exhausted and disillusioned, she decided to make one last grab at the real truth of life. She scraped together the remainder of her life savings, packed a few meager belongings, and headed for that last refuge of truth:

India.

India, she knew, was full of ashrams and gurus. What she wanted to find was *the* ashram and *the* guru of all gurus, the Supergu—the one person who knew the truth and who shared it with the rest of the world. It did not take long after her arrival in India to identify the Supergu of all gurus—he had a late-night talk show on Indian cable television.

The truth seeker traveled by train to a small village in southern India, and from there she took a four-wheel drive 40 miles, switched to a donkey for another 10-mile trek up the side of a remote mountain, and crawled on hands and knees the last 1,000 yards to the Supergu's ashram. To her dismay, thousands of other truth seekers were already ahead of her to see the Supergu. It was a long wait, with a long line, and she had to take a number as she had in Baskin-Robbins. She waited six days before they finally called her number. The assistant guru ushered her from the primitive dormitory, past the concrete lions representing confusion and paradox, and into a small, spare room. An old, bald-headed man sat on a pillow in the center of the floor, his legs crossed yoga-style, dressed in a sheet that resembled something from the sale table at a K-Mart. He smiled a lot, like children and all people who know the truth smile a lot.

The truth seeker walked contritely to the Supergu, bowed, and knelt trembling in front of him.

"How may I help you?" he asked in a gentle, grandfatherly voice.

"I am seeking the truth, your holy one. I wish to know why life works the way it does, what the principles of life are, why we are here, how I can take what I learn and apply it to my life and make my life work. Can you help me?"

The old man nodded solemnly.

"Then what is the secret?" she asked eagerly. "What's the real truth about life?"

The Supergu looked at her and said, "The truth about life—the only truth about life you will ever need to know—is, you are."

"I beg your pardon?"

"The only truth in life is, 'you are.'"

"I am what?"

"You and only you are you."

132

"I must be missing something in the translation. What do you mean?"

"The only truth is that 'you exist.' You are the center of your experience and you have lots of nows in your life. You are perfect, only you do not understand that."

"No, I certainly do not understand that. What do you mean, I'm 'perfect'?"

"You are unique. You are the only you. You are the perfect entity on this planet. You are the same yet different from everyone else. You are not perfect in the sense of being ideal, but you are perfect in the sense of being yourself."

The truth seeker stared at the Supergu in bafflement. Finally, after much effort, she said, "That's the biggest bunch of mumbo jumbo I've ever heard."

The Supergu kept smiling at her, like a person who has been insulted in a foreign language and doesn't know it. "You asked me for the truth. That is the truth."

"If that's the truth about life, it's ridiculous."

The Supergu kept smiling. She wondered how often he must brush his teeth a day. "Then I would suggest that you seek a second opinion," he said pleasantly.

The truth seeker left the ashram, deeply disappointed, and made her way to another ashram on the next mountain over, which the assistant guru had told her about. This ashram was not nearly as large as the first ashram and it had no assistant guru. It also had no waiting line. A large neon sign outside flashed on and off:

The Guru Is In

  The Guru Is In

    The Guru Is In.

The truth seeker walked right in and there sat the gu, also bald and also dressed in a K-Mart sheet. "How may I help you?" he asked her.

"I'm seeking the truth, your holy one. I wish to know why life works the way it does, what the principles of life are, why we are here, how I can take what I learn and apply it to my life and make my life work."

The gu motioned with his hand for her to sit in front of him. He nodded his head solemnly and said, "I think I can help you. But it will cost you."

Now she knew she was getting somewhere, for she had always known that truth would come at a price. She frantically dug into her purse and pulled out a plastic holder full of credit cards. "Master Card? Visa? American Express? Carte Blanche?"

The guru waved away her plastic. "No, it is not that kind of payment. If you really want to learn what the truth about life is, you must earn it."

Hesitating only a moment, the truth seeker agreed. "What must I do?"

"Did you see the barn on the way to my ashram?"

She had not only seen it, she had smelled it.

"That is where I keep my holy cows," he said. "I want you to go down to that barn and shovel all the cow dung out of that barn. Once it is cleaned out, I want you to keep it cleaned out. You will live here and keep that barn clean until I tell you the secret of life."

She looked down toward the barn and then back at the gu. "How long must I do that until you tell me the secret of life?"

"Ten years."

"Ten years! Holy cow!"

She almost left, but then thought that ten years of labor in the gu's barn would be worth the sacrifice if she would finally be able to learn the secret of life. So she went down to the barn and began shoveling out the cow dung. She shoveled month after month after month, year after year, until she became so good she was catching the stuff in midair.

Finally her ten years of labor were up and she went back up to the ashram to the guru. She knelt before him and said, "I have done what you required of me, master. Will you now tell me what is the truth about life."

The guru nodded solemnly, praised her for her diligent work in the barns, and said, "Yes, I will tell you. The truth about life is, 'you are.'"

She sat stunned. Then she screamed, "Wait a minute! That's exactly what the other gu told me ten years ago!"

The guru said, "That's right. And how much more crap are you going to shovel before you are going to get it?"

"Cogito, ergo sum (I think, therefore I am).
—*Descartes*

12

The Artichoke Syndrome

The concept of "I am" is not a provable truth. Philosophers will wrestle with that one a few more millennia. I know I am because I exist. When I go skiing where is the only place I fall? Here. With my body. I and only I experience my fall. I don't fall in somebody else's place, and nobody else experiences my falling, though they may empathize with me. I don't fall tomorrow or yesterday. I fall now. Here.

I am.

When I was in graduate school I had a rat named Thorndyke. Whenever I wanted to teach Thorndyke a certain behavior I put him in a maze with a piece of cheese down at the end of the fourth tunnel. Thorndyke would go down the first, second, third, and finally the fourth tunnel. After a while he skipped the first three tunnels and went right to the cheese. One day I took the cheese out. In time, Thorndyke realized what was going on and he quit going down the fourth tunnel. That's the difference between rats and humans. Rats learn after a while.

Humans, on the other hand, continue to play from effect instead of cause, avoid being home, clog their tubes with lies, limit their realities, and deny their personal responsibility for anything but the good stuff. Humans shovel the crap from one corner of the barn to the other for so long, in fact, that after a while it doesn't even feel half bad.

Why do we disavow the concept that *I am?* In my experience, most of us do so because we follow a pattern we learned from the time we were born:

We are here on earth to live up to the expectations of others.

We learned at an early age that what we believe to be true is not important. (Remember Our Lady of Perpetual Sorrow and

Guilt Forever?) What others think of us is. When we allow other people to hurt our feelings, for example, we are merely valuing their view of ourselves more than we value our own. Our cultural ethos dictates that our entire purpose on this planet is to seek the approval of others. We look to others to define our "I am." No wonder so few of us think we're the neatest thing since sliced bread.

A woman once told me she didn't like her job because her boss told her she was stupid, and she believed she was stupid because he told her she was. I said to her, if he told you to get down on all fours and turn your head sideways so he could pour a can of gasoline in your ear because he thought you were a car, would you? She replied indignantly, "No, that's ridiculous!" Then why, I said to her, do you believe you are stupid because he says you are?

Another woman I knew had a narrow-minded husband who frequently belittled her. She was approaching 40 and feeling insecure about it. But during her counseling with me and with her gynecologist we praised her for her looks and her spirit. She felt good about herself. One evening at home, she told her husband what I and the gynecologist had told her. The man replied contemptuously, "Did either one of them say anything about that forty-year-old ass of yours?" She said, "No, I don't believe your name came up at all.

We are here on this planet to live up to *our* expectations, and only our expectations.

Not that we should demean or ignore the observations, advice, and suggestions of others. But just as we should consult our memories and our belief systems, yet not let them run us, so should we listen to others.

"I appreciate your thoughts. Thanks for checking."

Learned at an Early Age

We learned to seek approval of others at an early age. We were walking around in this land of giants, and one day we picked up something the giants thought we weren't supposed to.

One of the giants came over and very subtly said, "DON'T TOUCH THAT! WHAT DO YOU THINK YOU'RE DO-ING!" The giant slapped our hand. We knew instantly we did not have the giant's approval, and as a child the one thing we most wanted, besides three square meals and clean diapers, was approval from the giants. The approval was especially important because it was always tied into love. When we did something good, we got hugs and kisses and were told how much the giant loved us. When we did something "wrong" we were told we were bad. We may not have always known what was right and what was wrong, but we sure were smart enough to seek that approval whenever we could.

As we grew older the reinforcement continued. Potty training was always a good one. The giants struggled with us on that one. We'd sit on the potty, butt hanging over the water, hands and elbows clinging to the seat, until one day something splashed in the water below, making us wet and cold, but the giants very happy. They immediately sent out fliers to the neigh-bors announcing D-Day, or Dump Day. Then the entire bath-room filled with giants, hanging from the curtain rod, cheering us on, yelling "Yeah, Teddy, come on, Teddy, give us a big poopoo," until we finally did, to the wild applause and cheers of the giants.

Approval continued in school, especially from the other kids, but also at home. In your house, were A's better than B's, C's better than D's? If you lived on earth they were. One semester I came home with all A's and one B. I proudly showed it to my dad and he pointed his finger to the B and said, "What happened here?"

If you want to see pressure for approval between parent and child, go to a Little League baseball game. I coached a Little League team once, and the pressure to win is enormous, espe-cially from the fathers (most of whom are vicariously trying to become through their youngsters the athletes they never were).

Don't we expect our kids to achieve certain goals, to be certain things? Aren't we disapproving if they flunk out of college (which we, not they, wanted them to go to) or settle into an occupation (or a series of occupations) that we think are below *our* expectations? If you have a bachelor's degree from college, don't you believe your children should have nothing less than a master's? If you don't have a college degree or a lucrative career, don't you "want something better" for you children? Not that there is anything wrong with encouraging and helping our children reach their fullest potential. That is a responsibility as a parent. But too often in the process we attempt to define for them what and who they should be. I've seen more than one family broken and divided because the parents did not "approve" of what their children were doing or who they were married to or where they lived.

We want our children to grow up independent, creative, imaginative, loving, and understanding that they can do anything they want to do in their life, that they hold the world in their hands. Yet when they start showing signs of that at age 13 we start calling them rebels and try to convince them to conform to our way of thinking.

The well-known writer and editor William Zinsser tells the story of his decision to become a writer. In the mid-1880's in New York City, Zinsser's grandfather had founded a prosperous factory that made shellac. His father had inherited the business, and it was expected that William, his only son, would continue the tradition. Yet Zinsser was determined to be a writer, and one day he told his father he had accepted a job on the *New York Herald Tribune*. His father accepted the decision with equanimity and wished him well. Zinsser recalled in his book, *On Writing Well:* "I was liberated from having to fulfill somebody else's expectations, which were not the right ones for me. I was free to succeed or fail on my own terms." How many parents are as equally gracious?

The striving for approval in the eyes of others never ceases: employees seek the approval from their bosses, bosses from boards of directors, politicians from the people, spouses from spouses.

It can also go to great extremes. One winter I was in Miami Beach—you know, God's waiting room, where everyone is cramming for their final exam. I'm walking along the beach on a 90° and 90 percent humidity day, and I see a woman, about my size and very round, lying on the beach in a string bikini. She oozed grease all over, as if somebody had dipped her in a can of Quaker State. She had a huge glob of white stuff on her lips, white plastic cups over her eyes, and another white glob on her nose— she looked like she had been to the Dairy Queen. She was lying on her back on a big towel, and her topside was beet red. I thought she had fallen asleep, so I walked up and said, "Excuse me. Hello."

"Yes?" she said.

"Ma'am, are you okay?"

"Of course I am. Why?"

"You must be in a lot of pain with that sunburn."

"Of course I'm in a lot of pain."

"Well, why are you doing that to you?"

"I'm from Pittsburgh."

"Ma'am?"

"I'm from Pittsburgh and today is the last day of my vacation. When I get home tomorrow my girlfriends are picking me up at the airport and when they take one look at me they're going to be so envious and so mad at me."

"You're going through all this pain to make your friends mad?"

"That's right."

"Ma'am, if you really want to make them mad have you thought about just going over to their place and crapping on their rug?"

The woman humphed, rolled over, and proceeded to toast her other side.

We even have songs that perpetuate this myth of the need for approval.

"People . . . people who need people."
"I can't stop loving you."
"You light up my life."
"You make me feel like a natural woman."
"If you ever leave me, I'm going to lay right down and die."

140

Thanks, but the last time I checked I was not on this planet to live up to your expectations and what you think about me. I am sure that if you were in my place you would do things differently, but as far as I can determine I and only I can occupy this space in this now, and thus only I can determine how I want to handle my nows.

You Are Perfect

We end up living our lives through others, not ourselves. We believe we need other people to feel good about ourselves, which is crap. You do not *need* anybody. You are. You are perfect. Wanting approval is acceptable and understandable. Needing it is not. You are the center of your experience. No one else can define or live your experiences for you.

But they try, don't they? Know any women who are 35 and unmarried? Notice how many of their friends and families don't consider them a whole person until they get married and have children? They may have a successful career and their own house and a dog and hobbies, but none of it counts. Notice how many of those unmarried women don't feel good about themselves because they aren't married? They've accepted society's dogma that a woman must be married before she can become a whole, happy, and desirable person. A woman, god forbid, who never marries becomes one of the ugliest words in the English language—a spinster.

And once you are married, you are expected to have kids. Anything less is high treason to the survival of the human species . . . this, despite the fact we have more people on the planet than the planet can comfortably support, or that some people do not want to have kids (and if they do have them because it is expected of them, what kind of parents are they apt to be)? I know a couple who has consciously chosen not to have kids . . . but they are seen as self-centered, and it is commented behind their backs that they'll be sorry when they get old because they won't have kids to take care of them. How nice it is for other people to decide that for them.

141

How many older women do you know—perhaps your own mother—who defined themselves through their children? When their children left the nest the women's lives suddenly were empty because they could not see themselves—and they felt others did not see or approve of them—except through the existence of their children. They can't wait for the birth of their grandchildren because they again have offspring with whom to redefine themselves.

Ever notice that while these critics are eager to tell you how *you* should be living, they seldom consult with you about how you think *they* should be living.

We are not on this planet to live up to the expectations of others. We do not *need* other people. Certainly most of us *want* other people. Most of us want to live with someone. Many of us want to have children. We find pleasure in that. But our desire to have a mate or to have children should always remain just that—our desire, not a need.

At age 13 I needed that approval. What others thought of me was important to me. Today, through a lot of experience and maturity, I have chosen to want to have people like me, to want to have them like what I wear and what I do and how I act. At 13 I needed it; now I want it. That is called growth. It is also called choice.

In American society we also have come to define ourselves through materialism. You are someone only if you own a certain car, use a particular brand of laundry soap, shop at the right stores, send your children to an influential college, wear the right clothes, travel to elite destinations, attend "in" culture events. More is better than less. Money is how we judge the game called Life, the yardstick with which we and others measure our "success." One million dollars is the magic number. The fact that many people do not find satisfaction in life—which I define as a function of our willingness to participate in life—has nothing to do with it.

Some people have taken the reverse tack. They've seen that the more-is-better-than-less philosophy often doesn't bring satisfaction, so they've adopted the less-is-better approach. This was popular in communes in the 1970's and is still popular among desert hermits and those die-hards who claim, "I got my jeep and my dog and that's all I need."

Scurvy Elephants

Either way, these people are defining themselves through external things and others' eyes. The result is we've become a nation of Pringles mentalities. You know Pringles, those artificial potato chips that come in a can? Pour a can out onto the table and you'll see that every one of them is identical. You won't find a blemish or a bubble or a brown spot among them. Toss a Pringle into a toilet bowl and it will blow up like a tortilla, and the grease will separate from the Pringle and climb the bowl for freedom. Me, I'll take a sack of Ruffles any day, with the burnt ones and the broken ones and the really perfect ones.

When I was in the third grade I came home crying after school one day. My mom asked me what was the matter and I said that I had heard the principal tell a teacher I was a scurvy elephant. "A what?" mom asked. A scurvy elephant. He called me a scurvy elephant. My mom immediately called the principal and demanded to know why he had called her son a scurvy elephant. "No, no, Mrs. Willey. That is just like Ted. He gets things mixed up sometimes. I did not call Ted a scurvy elephant. I said Ted Willey was a disturbing element."

We need more scurvy elephants in the world. We need more people who recognize that "they are" and that they do not need the approval of others to be. Scurvy elephants are doers. They are that small percentage of the population that plays Life from cause, who feel good about themselves, and who see themselves as capable of defining who they are instead of letting others do it for them. Doers don't always make the best decisions, but they own up to every decision they do make. They like risks and challenges. They're creative because they ask new questions and know they are the center of their experience.

Scurvy elephants are people who want to change the lyrics of those songs I mentioned earlier. The lyrics may not be as catchy, but the thoughts will be a lot more valuable.

"I can stop loving you; however, tonight I would rather not."
"If you should ever leave me . . . don't let the door hit you in the ass on the way out."
"You light up my life? Ha! *I* light up my life!"
"People . . . people who want people."
"You make me feel like a natural woman? *I* make me feel like a natural woman, and it has nothing to do with you."

The Artichoke Syndrome

This relentless quest for approval leads most of us to suffer from what I call The Artichoke Syndrome. Imagine yourself as an artichoke (or if you hate artichokes, think of yourself as an onion or a tree). The center of the artichoke—the center of us—is the meatiest, the tastiest, the tenderest, the most enjoyable part of the plant. Like the artichoke, we surround ourselves with protective leaves. These are our defense mechanisms, our rigid belief systems and mind sets, our excuse-making, our guilts, our worries, our living in the past or the future, our facades we show to seek the approval of others. As we grow older the leaves grow denser and tighter around our hearts, making it easier to receive approval or to weather the inevitable rejections we all receive from others who do not approve of the way we are living our lives.

The tighter the leaves, however, the less able we are to live in the now, to be responsible for our nows, to have the nows we truly want. Instead, we merely cope with the nows we experience because we let others decide our nows for us. The tighter the leaves the less we are able to be creative, imaginative, productive. Once we realize how unique each of us is, how we do not need the approval of others to be unique, then we can begin to peel away the leaves, exposing more and more of our heart, and in the process becoming more and more alive.

The closer we get to our heart, the greater the fear, stress, risk,

144

and vulnerability we face. But as we break through each layer we grow in our awareness, our aliveness, our alertness, our effectiveness, our confidence, our control, our reality. No pain, no gain as the saying goes.

While doing a seminar in New York City I met a woman who was terrified of living. She lived with her mother in Queens and had never traveled beyond Queens and Manhattan. She had no driver's license and had never flown in her life. But she told me she had always wanted to ski, so I encouraged her to come out to Colorado. No, no she couldn't afford that. I offered to put her up at my house and I would see that she would ski for free. No, no, she couldn't. The air fare was too—I offered to pay her air fare. No, no, she couldn't. She was frightened to fly. I suggested she take a train. In the end, she refused to come. It was just too frightening for her. She wouldn't leave her comfort zone; she wouldn't peel back some of those artichoke leaves she had wrapped so tightly around herself. Her life had reached a point of near paralysis.

While her refusal to leave her tiny world may seem unusual to most of us, her inability to peel back some of those artichoke leaves is not. Most of us in some way or another protect ourselves just as fiercely, whether it's not applying for a job we're "certain" we won't get, or not confiding in someone a personal problem, or telling a repairperson we won't accept the sloppy job that was done.

To be a doer in this world of critics, to live from cause instead of effect, to take charge of our lives, entails the risk and pain and fear (False Emotions Appearing Real) of peeling back those leaves and looking inward.

At a risk development group I was conducting for professionals, I asked one of the participants to go out and take a risk. The following week he told us what he had done. "I ride the bus downtown. Usually I sit toward the back and I rarely talk to anyone. So I decided to help the driver out by calling out the names of the streets as we passed them. I was kinda nervous at first. People looked at me real weird when I yelled 'Evans Avenue.' I think more people got off at that stop than normally did. I started to feel more confident, though, and I stood up and called out the next major street. People started to thank me, applaud. I met more people than ever on that bus. Some people began bringing wine and cheese. It was amazing.

As I said in the introduction, the core of this book is that for you to get more out of life you must always consult yourself. You know yourself best. To manage your employees you first must effectively manage yourself. To raise effective, independent children you first must be an effective, independent parent. To truly love your partner and your children and your friends you must first love yourself. Trying to live up to the expectations of others (and you never will succeed for critics are never satisfied) is self-defeating, for you are living your life through them. Indeed, in the long run attempting to please others all the time at the expense of yourself diminishes and sometimes destroys the very relationships you were trying so hard to satisfy. For living through others builds internal resentment and anger because you are not what you want to be. What most people do not realize is that it is really a lot easier (though sometimes scary peeling back those leaves) to be yourself. Being someone else is a lot of work.

A friend of mine named Sheldon Kopp wrote a book called, *If You Meet the Buddha on the Road, Kill Him!* What Kopp meant by that was, the world is full of Buddhas. If you are looking outside of yourself to find some meaning in your life, if you are trying to appease those Buddhas, you are looking in the wrong direction.

Most folks are about as happy
as they make up their minds to be.
                    —*Abraham Lincoln*

13

Travels to Bananaland

On September 1, 1983, Korean Air Lines Flight 007, while enroute from New York City to Seoul, Korea, strayed over Russian territory and was shot down over the Sea of Japan by a heat-seeking missile fired by a Soviet fighter-interceptor. All 269 passengers and crew on board, including 61 Americans, perished. All of them chose to die.

All 21 workers and patrons who were murdered at the McDonald's restaurant in San Ysidro, California, by James Huberty chose to die.

The seven shuttle astronauts chose to die.

My adopted son, Scott, chose to be born and chose to be physically abused by his biological parents.

Each of us is 100 percent responsible for everything that we experience in our lives.

Everything. We do not get to excuse our way out of anything . . . including birth and death.

This is usually the point in my discussions where I lose just about everyone. Most people can follow the principles of Total Responsibility Management up to a point. Once they begin to think about it, yes, they can see how they are 100 percent responsible for the failure of their marriage or the dead-end job they are in or the car wreck they experienced last week. But *choosing* to be born or to die—well, that's absurd. That's Bananaland. Even if you accept my definition of choice—not as want or wish but as conscious and unconscious decisions leading to consequences—the notion of choosing to die (not counting intentional suicides) rubs raw the core of our being. Why would the people at the McDonald's, many of them kids, have chosen to die? How could they possibly be responsible for their own deaths? James Huberty pulled the trigger. It just was their bad luck they happened to be there at the wrong time in the wrong place. There's no way they could have known, have predicted it, have foreseen it. Bad luck, not choice or personal responsibility.

Hey, and what about those 1,700 Africans who died when that lake in Cameroon quietly leaked toxic fumes one night and suffocated most of them in their sleep in their villages? Up until then the lake had been a lovely blue body of water the local residents called the "good lake." How could those people have "chosen" to die? It wasn't as though there had been some sort of warning they had ignored. It was, plain and simple, a freakish accident, an "act of God."

The outraged objections are understandable. Earlier I compared this book to a grocery store. You pick out what you want, what will best fit your needs. I firmly believe each of us is 100 percent responsible for every consequence in our life, and to accept less than that is to open the door to all those silly, paralyzing excuses we've been struggling so hard throughout this book to rid ourselves of. However, buying the notion that we choose birth and death, that we choose to be victims of "acts of God," does not negate the value of the rest of what we have explored. But bear with me in this chapter. In the act of entering Banana-land I think you will better understand the basic concepts of self-management. By reaching to understand these more extreme examples, you will have reached further than you would have otherwise. And by reaching, you will experience more satisfying, pleasurable nows than you ever had before.

I Shoveled a Lot of Crap

At age 31 I had everything I was supposed to have at that age: a wife, a child, a successful career as a manager with a large company—only I wasn't happy. My marriage wasn't working and my career wasn't providing the kind of satisfaction I was looking for. Like the truth seeker, I began to poke and prod among various religions and philosophies and books and gurus, looking for something to attach to, looking for something to run me. I shoveled a lot of crap in the process. I analyzed. I avoided. I reacted. I expected. I coped with my nows, shoveling from one corner of the barn to the other, throwing it out the window, moving it back and forth, using bigger and bigger shovels, but never resolving anything, never facing anything. I waited for the Supergu to arrive.

In time, I began to realize I was looking in the wrong places for the truth, that I simply needed to put my shovel down. I figured out what I needed to do was run everything through me and come up with something that was right for my needs. *I* was the one who had to determine what was right for me. I was the *only* one who could determine what was right for me.

I realized the word "guru" is spelled "gee . . . you . . . are . . . you."

What I came up with is what I call a self-management style, the tools necessary for me to manage me. That style I call *Total Responsibility Management*. TRM. It is based on "internality" and "causality," the concept that "I am," that I am the center of my experience, that I am the only one whose butt is in that chair, that nothing exists except to the extent that I choose to experience it.

On the ground floor the notion of being responsible for your own actions is pretty simple and pretty obvious. When you lock your keys in the car it's difficult to blame someone else, though people do try. When you push instead of pull, when you put the ice cream away in the refrigerator, when you forget someone's name, it is difficult to make excuses. I ran out of gas once smack in the middle of the Eisenhower Tunnel, a mile-and-a-half long tunnel that cuts through the mountains west of Denver. Running out of gas in the middle of a busy highway tunnel and trying to get some attention makes it difficult to keep your cool, especially when people are whizzing by you "signaling" their annoyance. Again, who was responsible? Did I choose to get in the car that morning? Did I assume the car had enough gas? Did I choose to drive up Interstate 70? Did I choose to drive through the tunnel instead of over Loveland Pass? No problem so far, right? No one else made those decisions for me, no one else did it to me. The car certainly did not do it to me. The car didn't care. The car would have sat in the garage all day and not whimpered once. I obviously did everything necessary to put myself inside the tunnel without enough gas. One might argue it was "bad luck" to have run out inside the tunnel and "good luck" if I had run out on the other side where I could have coasted all the way down to a gas station in Dillon. But the bad luck or good luck were still consequences of my actions.

What I had to wrestle with was when the consequences appeared to be more random or "beyond my control." All of us have experienced a flat tire at some point. Maybe it was as simple as a nail lying in the middle of the highway. You didn't even see the nail until you were forced to stop by the side of the road and inspect the tire. Did you choose to experience the flat tire? Did you create the "now" of the flat tire? Again follow the same unbroken chain of nows we went through when I ran out of gas in the tunnel. Did you choose to drive that day? Did you choose to take that particular route at that particular time? Did you choose to . . . ? No problems with accepting responsibility *up to the moment* your car ran over the nail? Any problem with accepting full responsibility if instead of the flat tire you had arrived safely and without delay at your destination? Yet the notion of taking personal responsibility for, choosing, authoring, or deciding to experience the now of the nail runs against common sense, doesn't it? It appears impossible to be able to foresee that a nail is lying on the highway and that it will pierce your tire. We recognize by now that the nail does not care, so we won't blame the nail. Bad Luck is probably the most obvious thing to pin it on. Bad Luck or Good Luck represent the randomness of the universe. They cause things to happen. They are the roll of the dice, the quirks of fate, the hit-or-miss. Two crossed stars put that nail there for you. The nail had your name on it (presumably written by someone or something else). But there is no way you could have caused yourself to have that flat tire, right?

The same thing with the people near the death lake in Cameroon or the patrons at the McDonald's or the passengers of Flight 007 or the people poisoned by pain relievers that had been tampered with. Yet . . . who chose to fly to Seoul? Who chose that particular flight (or let someone else select it for them)? Who chose to board the flight in New York or in Anchorage where they made their last refueling before being shot down? Everything's hunky-dory . . . up to the point when the Russians enter the scene. The Russians decided to shoot down the plane so they must be responsible. Yes, they were. They were 100 percent responsible. So were the passengers and the airliner's flight crew. Who put themselves in that position in the first place? Who suffered the consequences of their decisions?

Results do not lie.

James Huberty pulled the trigger at McDonald's. If he had not killed that day, would any of his "victims" have had trouble taking credit for going to the restaurant and eating lunch?

When things go well . . .

The difficulty, I realized, was if I accept the idea that something else causes me to experience that flat tire, then I have reopened the door to any and all excuses for all my experiences, especially the ones I don't like. I get to pick and choose, which is exactly what most people do today. What may be one person's responsibility is, in the eyes of someone else, a perfect excuse. To dismiss our accountability for the consequences of our actions in the case of the nail means a return to the arbitrariness that we have been attempting so hard to avoid in the first place. We've thrown consistency out the window. It means if people can decide when and when not to take responsibility for their actions, they can use any damn excuse they want any damn time they want. Being caught in traffic may not be an acceptable excuse to you, but it may be to someone who works for you or who was supposed to meet you for lunch. It means we get to take credit for the experiences we like and slough off the ones we don't like. It means when we play the game of Monopoly, some people can, if they choose, ignore the rules of the game and start with $2,000 instead of $1,500. If you are playing Monopoly with them, is that all right?

Many people contend that life's not fair in the first place. Some people start the game of Life with a helluva lot more than $2,000 and some start the game with zilch, so the rules don't mean much to begin with. Life's a flat bitch and death comes in the end anyway, so let's grease the skids and make the ride as fast and as easy as possible.

A friend of mine argues that my Bananaland extremes defy common sense, practicability, and most of all, "reality." I'm ignoring the complexities of life, he argues vociferously. No person can foresee, let alone avoid, all the bad events a person will experience, whether it is a flat tire or eating at McDonald's the day James Huberty walks in carrying three guns.

I agree none of us can foresee clearly the future. That's what makes life exciting instead of predictable and dull. A self-management style, while providing far more of those pleasurable nows than we once experienced, will not make all the nows we have ones we want or desire. But even with the ones we don't like, taking responsibility will help us understand and learn from them and continue to grow.

Each of us has nows to experience on this planet. For some of those nows we are conscious, awake, and anticipate them occurring; we make decisions or choices about each of them. In other situations, we delegate our nows or the results of those nows to someone else. The results may be desired or not desired. But life works only forward. We make the best possible decisions for each now with the tools we have. Either way, notice that the results of what occurs is exactly the same.

There may have been a genuine intention of the people on Flight 007 to die. People get what they choose to get. That's why results do not lie. That is not a comforting, acceptable, or understandable concept to most of us. Who would choose to experience something so tragic or painful, and without benefit? I have no answer to that. I can't say why someone would choose to be blown away while eating a hamburger. But merely because we do not understand or desire some of our nows does not negate our personal responsibility for them.

I am concerned about our becoming preoccupied about accepting the "perfection" of it all, about constantly wondering "why" something happens to us. Millions of dollars and who knows how much time and research have been spent on analyzing that stuff.

People meet every Friday afternoon at their local bars for their "why me" groups. They want to shovel that shit from one corner of the barn to the other. It is a waste of time. It is a preoccupation with the past and the future. Life is too short for that stuff. Whatever my choices are, I must take the consequences for them, including the fact that I may put myself in a position that results in ultimate pain.

What you can gain from accepting complete responsibility, and the consequences that go with it, is that you will—I guarantee that you will—experience more satisfying nows along the way than you ever had before. Many more. And when those consequences come along that you don't want and don't understand you will more readily accept them.

While an extremely elusive idea to grasp, it is not always so complex as we might think. Several years ago 84 people made the interesting choice to die in the MGM Hotel fire in Las Vegas. Life's a bitch, right? Yet look what happened in the aftermath of that fire, at least for a while. Guests at hotels began bringing smoke alarms in their briefcases, rope in their luggage. They counted the number of doorways from their room to the fire escapes. People refused to stay above three. People who booked conferences sent their lead people to check the fire prevention facilities. Did these people choose *not* to die in a hotel fire? And what about those who did not choose to take simple precautionary measures, or forgot about them as time went on, not wanting to appear to be paranoid? Ninety-six of them chose to die several years later in a hotel fire in Puerto Rico. The hotel had no sprinkler system and no smoke alarms in the rooms. Bad Luck?

What I came to realize as I too struggled with this difficult concept is that nobody knows what reality is. As we discussed earlier, reality is what each of us makes for ourselves, and that reality can expand and change each day for us if we are willing to let it. Reality is limitless. The complexities of that reality change too. What once was complex becomes simple as our reality expands, just as mathematics becomes less complex and mystifying for us as we study it. Some hotel guests in the wake of the MGM fire expanded their reality. And where does one draw the line on complexity? Is there a quotient of complexity at which point each of us is dismissed from personal accountability? Nails on highways meet the quotient, but ringing telephones do not?

If life could be run backwards, we could ensure that all turns out well. Or if we all could agree on a single judge to rule on these cases, and we all agreed to abide by the judge's rulings, it might work. God is the closest I know to such a judge, and there certainly is little agreement about who he or she is or how much God dabbles directly in the affairs of humans. Besides, if it is your butt in that chair do you really want someone else making your decisions for you?

More Bananaland

I said at the beginning of this chapter that my son Scott chose to be born and he chose to be beaten and battered by his biological parents. The concept of choice is especially difficult with children, for choice implies some ability to reason, to make rational, informed decisions. Yes, we can choose to get on or not get on a particular plane or we can avoid fast-food restaurants or we can take our smoke alarms to the hotel; but a child, a child can't do these things. We have the same view toward the mentally ill; a schizophrenic is no more able to make rational choices than a child. But I believe we are confusing body and mind with spirit. Remember, I said we are our spirit, our being, our essence, our force, our soul first, and we have a body and mind as tools to use while we're on earth.

I suggest that your spirit, your essence, has always been and always will be. Your spirit chooses when to be born and it chooses when to die. It takes physical form for its short stay here on earth. To my way of thinking, the seven shuttle astronauts chose to die and are having a helluva party on the other side. Death is saving the best for last.

Not everyone subscribes to this philosophy, or some would say, religion. Whether you do or do not is less important than recognizing that while you are here on earth you do have the tools to make choices and that you are shortchanging yourself if you do not avail yourself of them.

I am important and you are important.
If I devalue you, I devalue myself.
                    —Thomas Harris

14

Circle of Responsibility

We have looked at who we are, how we operate principally from effect instead of cause, and how we got that way. We've looked at what each of us can do to take control of our own lives, how we can more consciously and deliberately be responsible for our behavior and actions. We've learned how to better manage ourselves. Now the tough part: how do we make this work in a world that does not understand and operate from—indeed, will likely resist—total responsibility management? If I'm 100 percent responsible for my own actions, what about all those other people?

The first step is to stop thinking of them as *others*. You know you create your own reality. You are the center of your experience. Other people do not do it to you or create your reality for you. You are, in essence, creating all these people in your life all the time. You chose to be born to certain parents (you can slough that one off). You chose to marry a certain person, work for a certain boss, have certain kids. You created those people in your reality. The result is you and a bunch of other "you's" in your reality. Each person you create in your experience is a *reflection* of yourself.

Everybody is us.

Is this more mumbo jumbo, Ted? It may sound that way, but let's go back to that blue Monday *aha* you experienced earlier in the book. It's gray and cloudy and you know—you just know—you're going to have a rotten day. You come down to the breakfast table and here come the kids.

"Haven't you gone to school yet! Make your bed! You can't

156

wear that to school! No, you can't eat any more junk cereal! Watch your mouth! I brought you into this world, I can take you out!"

Now it is Friday. Sunny, payday, a three-day weekend coming up, lunch out with an old friend. Kids come down to breakfast.

"Good morning, kids. Let me give you a big hug and kiss. No, I don't think that's an appropriate dress to wear to school, Jill. Let's pick out something together. We're having eggs today; tomorrow you can have cereal. Have a good day at school."

Sound familiar? Ever notice that your experience of your children, or other people, has a lot to do with *your* attitude? They are mirror images of you. Not perfect, of course. My kids want junk cereal every day. My kids can get wild and angry even when I'm not. But if I am in a cooperative mood, they are more apt to be in a cooperative mood. If I am in control of myself, they are more apt to be in control of themselves.

Have you ever gone to a dog show? Check out the pets and their masters. Talk about reflection. They not only look alike, they have similar temperaments and attitudes. Mirror image. Or a couple who has lived together for a long time and who look exactly alike: same clothes, same pet phrases, same appearance, same mannerisms. Or a home—you can almost immediately tell something about other people when you walk into their home.

Your entire world reflects you.

I've conducted exercises with individuals to illustrate this principle of reflection. The participants pair off and face each other sitting in chairs. I dim the room lights, get everyone relaxed, and then ask them to roll back down the ladder of their minds all the way back to first grade. I ask them to think of who their best friend was then. What was his or her name, what did they look like? What did they find in that friend that was special? What attracted them to that friend? Then I ask them to think about someone they did not like. What was it about that person they did not like? I repeat this process for two or three more grades, through high school. I also ask them to remember their favorite teachers along the way and what it was about those teachers that they most liked or admired.

Repeat this process yourself. Think back to first grade, junior high, high school. Spend a little time and remember.

Once everyone has finished, I ask them to recall to their partner their memories, who they liked and why, who they did not like and why. When we are through with that we discuss their memories with the group at large. It soon becomes apparent that for most of us our friends and nonfriends reflect aspects of ourselves. What we see in our friends and our teachers that we like is that part of us we like or would like to be; what we see in people we do not like is that part of us we do not like or do not want to become.

This response is not as surprising as it first appears, since students of human behavior have long contended that within each of us lies the potential to be loving, cruel, weak, strong, alert, *unc,* confident, anxious—all the palette of human behavior. Each of us display or suppress these character traits in different ways, to the point we are as individual as fingerprints, and we are attracted or repelled by people who display a similar balance of traits. Being a perfect human being is the paradox of being unique, yet simultaneously the same as other human beings.

As a child I stole. Most of us probably did too, at least once or twice, just to try it out. I used to take my dad's change from his dresser, just a little bit so he wouldn't notice. Then I moved onto candy bars in stores and by the time I was thirteen I was stealing that infamous magazine, *Sunshine and Health* (photos of men and women playing volleyball at nudist colonies). I have since grown very uncomfortable with people who steal, for I see within them my past behavior and my present potential to steal.

Grasping the concept of reflection is important, for the art of stimulating other people also to be responsible 100 percent of the time corresponds directly to our ability to communicate and tap (mainly through modeling) that part of people most like ourselves or most what we want to be. If I am 100 percent responsible for my behavior and actions, then those other "me's" around me are more apt also to be 100 percent responsible because they are responding to my positive behavior.

The Mirror of Ourself

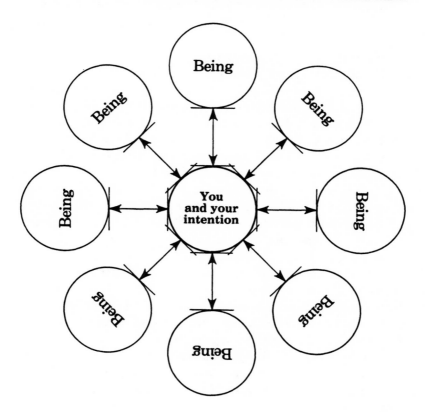

Intended Intentions

Notice in the center circle of the Mirror of Ourself illustration the phrase "You and your intention." Between you and me is intention. Intention is the energy that precedes the act of deciding or choosing. Each now in life is preceded by an intention to experience that now. For example, between you and me is an intention to read this book. Or you have an intention to have a drink with a friend or conclude a business deal or eat breakfast or get married or have healthy children or whatever other nows are filling your life. Many times an intention is unconscious. We may not understand why we intended to do what we did. Like choice, however, we still remain responsible for the intention.

My intention is my experience.

My experience is my intention.

When someone wins a lottery, and it comes as a complete surprise, did they intend to win? They may say no, I just thought I'd take a chance. I think they intended to win—that is, they intended to do everything necessary to contribute and then sit back and hope and wish. And when they won, obviously they intended to win because that was their result.

If someone dies in your family, did you intend for them to die? No. You didn't want or wish that they would die. You didn't physically cause them to die. Did you intend to experience the now of experiencing someone dying in your family? Yes. Your experience is your intention.

Intention is a very difficult concept, yet it is so critical because it has to do with people becoming clear in their own mind as to what their intentions are going to be. What is someone's intention when he or she applies for a job and goes into the interview half-baked, unconfident, hoping, wishing?

Often when I am before a group of adults I ask for a show of hands of those who have been divorced. As you might expect, a large percentage usually have been. How soon in that relationship, I ask them, did you know you did not *intend* to make the relationship work? For people who have never been divorced, the response can be rather startling. Nearly every time one and often more people respond that they knew their marriage was not going to work *before* they got married. "While walking down the aisle," people have told me.

For me, I knew my first marriage was not going to work two days before we were married, though it took us ten more years before we actually signed the divorce papers. At the time I got married I had just flunked out of Ohio State University, lost any chance of a football or wrestling scholarship, faced the Vietnam draft, and needed maturing. I was changing addresses as fast as I could. My future wife had just graduated and was working as a social worker in Columbus. Marrying her would defer me for a while, she had a job, and her parents wanted us married. It seemed like a good idea at the time. Did I intend to get divorced? No! I intended for the relationship not to work.

Intention is how we go into a situation. Ever drive a new car into a supermarket parking lot? A spot—your parking place—is up front, but you say to yourself, No, I better park way out in the lot so my door won't get dinged. Oh, hell, I'll only be a minute. You park in front, come out a minute later, and sure enough, the door is dinged. You not only chose to have your door dinged, you intended to. You must have. Results don't lie.

Like choice, we can carry intention into Bananaland. Not only did the people who died at the San Ysidro McDonald's choose to die, they intended to die. The people who died on the DC–10 that crashed at O'Hare Field intended to crash. They intended to get up that morning, intended to get on the plane, intended to take the seat assigned, intended to experience all the nows to the takeoff point. No problem up to the moment of the crash understanding the word intention. But that is where people balk.

Yet, I never hear anyone say, I do not intend for my marriage to be working, I did not intend to have healthy children, I did not intend to be enjoying the job I have, I did not intend to make budget. I did not intend to arrive safely on the flight. The only time we have problems is with the negative, the undesirable results. We have a difficult time giving people permission to make decisions we would not make if we were them.

Modeling Our Behavior

Now that we understand reflection and intention, what do we do with them? How do we make them work for us in a world that does not understand? If the people around us reflect what we intend, making total responsibility management work is a matter of us simply doing what we want to have done to us. If you are standing in front of a mirror, you get back what you put out, unless you're standing in front of an amusement park fun mirror. If you want those around you to start taking complete responsibility for themselves (kids, employees, friends, service people), then *first* you must take responsibility for yourself. You must set the example. You must provide the leadership.

Think of it this way. If you want your children to tell you the truth all of the time you must first believe that truth is important. You then must act and behave in a truthful manner . . . 100 percent of the time. You do this so that your children see that your beliefs (which you've no doubt preached to them dozens of times) are not only in your mouth but in your actions. For you to get the truth back from your children, you yourself must first act and tell the truth. This is called modeling. The story of the boy who cried wolf is a parable about the consequences of modeling certain behavior. He got back what he put out.

Recently I was driving the Interstate with my son Scott, who at the time was taking driver's education. I'm tooling along when Scott says,

"Dad, you're speeding."

"It's okay. Fifty-five is a joke."

"Can I speed then?"

"No. I've driven a lot more than you, Scott. I'm more mature."

"You're still over fifty-five, dad."

"Son, the man mowing the right-of-way is going faster than I am."

It is often said you cannot love someone else unless you love yourself first (this does not mean you must approve or love all of your behavior). That may sound like psychological double-talk or narcissism. But think of it from a different perspective. Think of all the people you know fairly well—relatives, friends, co-workers—and think of the ones you really like. Do you not tend to like the people who most love themselves? I don't mean superficial love . . . people who are narcissistic, arrogant, self-indulgent, vain (below the surface these people are insecure and self-hating). I'm talking about confident, self-respecting, proud, in-charge people, people who may not like everything they do but who believe and act as people deserving of fair treatment and respect from others. Don't you find it easier to like or love those people? Don't they make the most effective and productive co-workers, the most fun friends, the most endearing relatives? Aren't they the people you most want to hang around with, who you most want to know and work with? They most readily project self-love and they most readily get love back. They manage themselves, and others see and respond to that positively. They're the kind of people who have lots of friends and lots of support from family. They are the kind of people who become leaders, whom people go to for counsel.

Men who beat their wives or girlfriends are not men who love themselves, are confident about themselves, who see themselves as "perfect" individuals. They cannot get love by projecting love, so they attempt to get love by trying to control their partner through psychological and physical intimidation. They fail, and thus get back, in a different form, what they put out. Typically the woman who puts up with this battering for long also does not love herself, feels inferior, and lacks self confidence. She too gets back what she puts out. (As an aside, for all those who want to put all the blame on one or the other party, both are in fact 100 percent responsible for their experiences.)

How many times have you gone to a conference or heard a speaker or read a book that excited and *motivated* you? No, it did not. You motivated yourself. You chose to allow yourself to feel motivated. Later you may have complained that the program or the book was fine, but it didn't last. Now you are making the program responsible, when in fact you chose to no longer feel motivated. Thank you, but do not make others responsible for your decision to stop being responsible for yourself.

As I suggested earlier, I believe one major reason the world has come to play so much from effect instead of cause is because our political leaders, our parents, our preachers, our teachers, our role models, preach and advocate and counsel us as children to be responsible for our own actions, yet themselves constantly find fault and bitch and blame and shirk responsibility when it suits them. Look around today and you will discover it is difficult to find people willing to take responsibility for their good—*and bad*—consequences. Yet these same people constantly express their annoyance at their children who lie, their employees who come in late, their friends who don't come through when they need them.

Circle of Responsibility

What the critics of the world do not understand is they cannot force others to act. If each person is 100 percent responsible for his or her own actions, then only that person can choose how he or she will act and behave. Only on the planet Uranus can a parent "make" their child not lie. In the same vein, you cannot force the rest of the world to be 100 percent responsible. In fact, in light of the way the world operates today, the harder you attempt to preach 100 percent responsibility the less likely you are to succeed. Modeling is the only effective way to make this work. And the way to model is through what I call the Circle of Responsibility.

At the top of this circle is what I call "Our Beliefs." I believe in telling the truth, I believe in being on time for all commitments, I believe in accepting 100 percent responsibility for my actions (or the converse of these beliefs or any other beliefs you want to plug in.) This is the "me" in life. I must start with me because it is the only thing over which I have absolute control.

At three o'clock on the circle you see "Our Behavior." My beliefs and attitudes have an impact on how I choose to behave and act. My behavior and actions and attitudes have an impact on how other people perceive me. How they perceive me affects their own beliefs and attitudes (six o'clock). That is, what I do may reinforce, repel, or change how they view themselves and the world about them.

The Experience of Other People

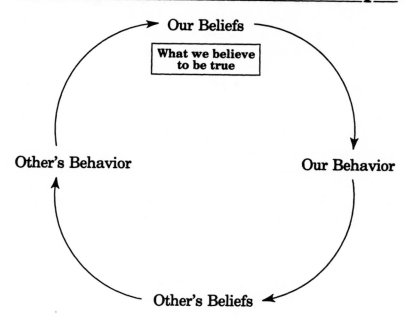

Now the critical part. Other people's beliefs about me have an impact on their behavior *when they are dealing with me* (nine o'clock). The impact, of course, is not always direct or obvious, nor is it necessarily 100 percent. But it does have an impact. I have incorporated in my belief system that telling the truth is important and absolute. I have communicated that verbally and modeled it through my behavior to my children. They understand that I not only tell the truth at all times but that it is important to me I receive the truth at all times. Consequently, when they deal with me they are more apt—after continued reinforcement—to tell me the truth at all times.

As you might expect by now, the impact of your behavior on others increases if your behavior is *consistent.* That is a critical word: consistent. If you lie often to or in front of your children, then the few times you do tell the truth is not going to affect them much. Your behavior and attitudes must be cumulative. People who see you consistently arrive to work on time or consistently keep agreements or consistently take responsibility for your actions are more apt to respond to you in like manner. Or vice versa. I know a woman who works for a man who is never on time for anything. His lateness is a standing joke among the people who work for him. They plan to arrive late for meetings he has scheduled since they know he won't be there at the appointed hour. When he requests reports in by a certain time, his staff ignores him. He gets back what he puts out.

To finish off the Circle of Responsibility, how other people behave with me has an impact on what I choose to believe about them, and consequently, how I act toward them. If they are consistently late for appointments, for example, or fail to produce the agreed-upon results, then my behavior is that I will no longer do business with them.

Driving the Circle Backwards

Unfortunately, most of us most of the time are out to change the other person first. "I'm your father and you'll do what I say because I say it." "I'm in charge around here and this is the way you'll do it." We expect more out of others than we are willing to give out of ourselves. We try to change others not by changing ourselves first, but by driving the Circle of Responsibility *backwards*. But that is impossible, isn't it? As we've already concluded, you can only be responsible for your own attitudes, behaviors, and actions; you cannot be responsible for anyone else's. To change others, they must see a change in our behavior first.

While putting on a program for a five-star hotel in Florida, I was walking along a corridor one day with the president. A cigarette butt on the floor caught his eye and he said to me, "I'm going to get one of the maids up here to pick that up," and he walked on. I picked up the butt and put it in my pocket and walked on with him to his office, where he immediately called the head of staff and said, "There's a cigarette butt on the floor near room three-ten. Get a maid up there right away." About that time I held the cigarette butt up and the president said on the phone, "Never mind."

After he hung up I told him that as president he was just as responsible as his maids for the cleanliness of his property. He should have picked up the butt himself and his telephone call should have focused on making the staff more alert to such items in the future. Leaving the butt there and demanding that a maid go up and get it leaves the wrong impression.

Modeling is Hard Work

Most of us try to drive that Circle backwards because, frankly, it's just damn easier to do it that way. It is easier to tell someone what to do than to do it ourselves. It is easier to tell your kids to clean up their own room than it is to clean up yours. To model Total Responsibility Management means you must build from the inside out, and that's hard work. Modeling is not glamorous or power-oriented or quick. It is not as simple as preaching or redrawing the company organization chart. My guess is that part way through this book you began thinking of someone *else* you thought should read this book so they could get *their* act together.

Our behavior usually correlates to our habits, and habits typically have been ingrained in us from an early age. Can we change a habit now? No. Can we change pieces of our behavior? Yes. And what is a habit but a string of pieces of behavior.

Modeling does work. I know a man who is an editor of a magazine. One day he called an author, whom he had never met, to go over some changes he had made while editing the author's article and to request that the article be retyped. The author indignantly refused. He bitched that he had just had another article badly edited at another publication, and that if anything was touched in this article for any reason he would refuse to allow the magazine to run the piece. The editor remained calm, pointing out that some editing was required for the article to conform to the magazine's style and to improve readability. He offered to run the changes by the writer. The writer angrily refused and hung up.

Two hours later, the writer called back, apologized for his childish behavior, and said that he, the editor, "seemed like a good fellow." Subsequently, the author assisted the editor in every detail to ensure that the article was ready for publication. Note that the editor did not choose to plug into the author's anger. Instead of blowing up at the author, he "modeled" calm, confident behavior. He remained conscious. He avoided telling the author how to behave or where to stick it. And he got back what he put out. What would have happened if he had plugged into the author's anger? Do you think the author would have called back to work cooperatively with the editor?

The next time you go to a restaurant, try modeling the kind of service you want. You know what usually happens at a restaurant: "Hi, my name is Alf and I'll be your waiter tonight." That's the last time you'll see Alf until he brings the bill. When I find a waiter providing slow service I might ask if he is having a bad day. Or I will say up front that we're not in a hurry tonight, that I'm interested in having a pleasant dining experience. I might ask him his name first, how long he's been working here, how's the evening been going. I model pleasantness and consciousness (how many diners are as *unc* as their waiters?), and in return I nearly always get better service.

Modeling does not work 100 percent of the time. If I am the manager of five people, I can project motivation by being motivated myself. I can create an atmosphere for motivation. I can show consistency, effectiveness, respect, eye contact, being home. But I cannot *make* those five people be motivated. I cannot tell them to be motivated and expect that to do the trick. Motivation is internal, not external. They must motivate themselves, and the best I can do is to make it clear to them through my actions that self-motivation is a value that I hold dear. Some of them will respond; some will not.

Although I cannot guarantee modeling will work all the time,

168

I can guarantee that if you don't first model the behavior you desire, you not only do not have the right to expect others to model it, they will not model it. I know of no other effective, long-lasting way to get people to change their behavior.

Though I am different from you,
we were born involved in one another.
                                    —Tau Ch'ien

15

Life Games

If modeling is the key to making 100 percent total responsibility living workable in a world that functions predominately from effect, then how can I make modeling work more effectively? How can I help others get more in touch with their own sense of responsibility?

Let's examine first how we spend our time. We have only 24 hours in each day, and if we are going to start doing things differently in the world, then we need to look at how we are spending those 24 hours. We talked earlier about how little most of us are "home" each day and the value of living in the now more often. Nowhere are we more frequently on vacation than in our relationships with other people. The following is a look at six ways of how we interact with others. It ranges from the extreme of Withdrawal to the most conscious state called Genuineness. As an individual progresses from Withdrawal to Genuineness there is greater associated risk—and with it greater rewards.

Structuring Time

I. WITHDRAWAL

This condition takes place when an individual escapes from the present, often physically as well as psychologically. Senility, infantile autism, schizophrenia, and alcoholism are more extreme forms of withdrawal. The artichoke leaves don't get any tighter than this.

170

More common forms of withdrawal can be watching television or sleeping or daydreaming. When I do not want to be here, when I want to escape, I sleep. We all want that escape now and then, however much in control of life we feel. But too often people sleep to avoid life altogether. Do you know people who sleep ten, twelve, fourteen hours a day? If you have teenage children you do. They sleep forever. It is one way of escaping the tribulations of adolescence. My grandmother does not want to be here, either; she sleeps 15 hours a day—12 hours at night and a 3-hour nap each afternoon. Sleeping involves zero risk, short of the house burning down while you are dozing.

I notice when I am willing to participate in life, to play more from cause instead of effect, I do not require as much sleep because I want to be conscious more. I don't want to miss out on life's experiences. Why would I? I choose them. If you sleep seven or eight hours or nine hours a night now, try cutting back gradually. You will find that you will do just fine on less sleep than you thought possible.

II. RITUALS

If you are awake and around other people, you will encounter the Rituals. Rituals are predictable, unconscious experiences people have at work or socially, often when they meet. You pass someone in the hallway. Hey, great to see you . . . how you doing? . . . let's have lunch sometime . . . see you later. This is a ritual because (1) it's not great to see them, (2) you don't care how they are doing, (3) you don't intend to have lunch with them ever, and (4) you hope never to see them later.

Life is full of these little encounters. How are you? . . . Thanks for calling . . . Have a nice day . . . We've got to get together . . . Hiwhat'syournamewhatdoyoudowhereyoufrom? . . . What sign were you born under? . . . Haven't we met? . . . Who's your role model? . . . How's the weather? . . . Have a good one . . .

Rituals are a good place to start out helping others get conscious. Next time somebody says, "Hi, how about lunch?" you reply, "No thank you. "That will get the other person conscious quickly. If you prefer something less blunt, make your usual statements and replies, but try to be more genuine. Get eye contact and be conscious. If you say, "Hi, how are you?" mean it and show it.

Rituals are not always verbal, either. As I suggested earlier, try sleeping on the other side of the bed or sit in a different chair at the dinner table. Break the routine! Try making love at a different, more spontaneous time. Families,especially, get into a rut of mindless activities. Some go so far as preparing the same meals the same nights of every week. Companies get into ruts, doing the same job the same way, day in and day out. The weekly planning meeting is held precisely at 10 o'clock every Monday, whether there is anything to plan or not. Routine serves a useful purpose; too much routine kills creativity, initiative, aliveness. Variety is not only the spice of life, it gets people alert, and people alert are more apt to be responsible.

Your initiative and creativity in upsetting these daily rituals that keep so many of us *unc* is frequently the first step towards modeling that behavior you want to convey to them. People you've made conscious by upsetting their routine will take notice of you, and once you've gotten their attention they will see you modeling that playing-from-cause approach to life.

III. ACTIVITIES

Activities are those mindless chores and routines we go through every day, at work and at home. Cooking meals, cleaning house, going to meetings, writing reports, holding the stop sign at road construction sites. People who hate their work go *unc* when they arrive at the office; others go *unc* only at home.

IV. PASTIMES

These wasters of time and closeness typically involve social situations, usually of a little more depth than rituals, ideally preceding moving into substance. They are a way to communicate, yet remain *unc* at the same time.

What did you do in the war? . . . Where do you get your hair done? . . . Where do you shop? . . . What kind of car do you drive? . . . Who's your gynecologist? . . . Did you see the Celtics play last night? . . . Would you like to see a picture of my

172

children? . . . You shoulda seen what Billy did the other day . . . Yes, that is cute, but you shoulda seen what Ryan did . . .

I once watched three men at a party sitting silently together. Finally one of them, in whose home the party was being held, said, "Did I show you guys my new shop tools?" The other two men replied yes, he had. The first man said, "Do you want to see them again?"And all three went down to the basement.

This small talk is initially fine when you meet someone, but unless you want to remain unconscious you need to then move on to more genuiness with others to get more genuine, substantive results.

V. GAMES

Much of our time every day involves playing games, at work and in our personal lives. Games are used to avoid being genuine, to avoid risk, to avoid taking responsibility for one's own actions. They are power plays, an attempt to drive that Circle of Responsibility backwards. Often they are the result of unconscious habits. They usually are confrontational and destructive to one or more participants. They involve making someone else wrong and spreading bad feelings. Some individuals become so adept at playing games they are known as "advanced game players."

There is the boss who says, "You're 82 cents off on your budget calculations. Find it! "Or the supervisor who says, "I know you've already got a load of work, Alan. But this report has to be done immediately. Of course, if you can't do it, I'll find somebody else who can. "And we all know colleagues or friends who set up fights by saying, "Helen said you did . . . "There is the guilt seeker who in essence says, "See the bags under my eyes? You did that to me. "Or the individual who seeks our sympathy by letting us know that, "I don't feel very well today, and my car wouldn't start and my kids are giving me fits and my boss doesn't understand me and . . .

Which of these games do you play? Pick three games you like to play. Think about them. How can you change your participation in those games? How can you change the participation of others around you in those games? Your ability to spot these games and break them up is fundamental to changing the world around you. Some of these games can destroy a marriage or a company or a friendship.

VI. GENUINENESS

This is the one that requires the highest risk. To be genuine you must be here now, you must peel back the leaves of the artichoke and expose yourself, you must share your feelings with others. Genuine people author their own experiences, accept others the way they are, and do not feel fearful or jealous, but are confident and loving.

Loving is defined as giving people the space to be who they are and who they are not . . . yet. It is accepting each person as "perfect." Love is not being jealous. It has been said that jealousy is the jaundice of the soul. Love is not ownership. If you love someone, it does not mean you own them. Whenever you are jealous of someone else, you are demeaning yourself. Why would you want to demean yourself?

Coming to the Rescue

One of the best ways to help others get in touch with themselves is to stop rescuing them. Most typically, we rescue our children. Yet, there is an important difference between being responsible for your child and being responsible for your child's responsibility. Legally, you have certain responsibilities. If your child takes your car and runs into someone, you are going to be held legally accountable. Your child, however, is responsible for his or her responsibility, and must pay the consequences.

As a parent it is important to ask, "Is my child asking for or doing something I don't think is responsible for me as a parent to let my child do?"If your answer to that is yes, then you have a responsibility to correct the situation. If, on the other hand, your child is asking you to do something you would not do *if it were you,* then you have a different situation. Then you need to clarify with your child the potential consequences of his or her actions. Then I think you have a responsibility as a parent to let them choose or not choose to do it. Why? To begin with, you are not them. You cannot experience their experiences. You cannot make their choices for them. If you do, you are rescuing them. Allowing them to make their own decisions is a way for them to grow up, to mature, to learn independence. Too often parents hover over their children and fail to allow them the freedom of making choices and experiencing the good—and bad—consequences of those choices.

My son wanted to buy a set of drums. I knew it wouldn't last. I knew it was something I wouldn't do if I were him. But it was his money, and once I outlined the consequences I let him go. The drums lasted three months and are now in his closet. That's called learning, and there is no faster way to learn than by experience.

Use common sense when approaching these situations. If your spouse is unfairly disciplining one of your children, do not rescue the child. As soon as possible, talk privately to your spouse. Work out the mutual rules about discipline or about the spouse's behavior. Perhaps your spouse chose to have a bad day at work and took it out on the child. Then it is the responsibility of that spouse, not you, to rectify matters with the child. Common sense says that if that spouse should start physically abusing the child, then you do indeed need to intervene, just as you don't let your child get run over in the street just to prove to him there are definite consequences to his being *unc.*

Let's review this again: Either you are deciding what you think is responsible for you as a parent to let them do or not do, or you are deciding if they are asking or doing something you would not do if you were them. Those are the only two options a parent has. Now this obviously is a judgment call. No two people are going to always agree into which category your child's request has fallen. But examine closely before you make such a decision whether in fact you are rescuing your child. Let's quickly look at a few examples of what I mean.

- Clothes are always fun. I think most of us would agree it is a parent's responsibility to provide their children with adequate clothing. But is it your responsibility to select every single item they wear on a particular day? What parent hasn't faced a child who wants to go to school wearing a combination of clothes that could only be appropriate for Halloween? Isn't your demand that they wear what *you* want merely an example of you asking them to not do something you would not do *if you were them*?

- You are in a store with your six-year-old. Your child has a dollar she earned doing chores for you, and the child wants to spend it on something. She picks out an item that obviously is a piece of junk and will be lucky to last the night before falling apart. The temptation for most parents is to say no. But again you are telling her not to do something you would not do if you were her. But you are not your child. Explain to your child that you think the item is not well built and will not last, and that the money would be better spent on something else. If your child still wants to buy it (and don't they always), let her. If it falls apart, perhaps next time she will choose more wisely.

- Your 15-year-old daughter wants to stay out until midnight on school nights. As a parent, it seems to me you have a responsibility in this case for the welfare of your child. She isn't asking to mix plaids and stripes. Setting a time limit and doing all you can to enforce it is your responsibility as a parent. Your child's decision to obey or defy that limit is her responsibility. Conveying that can be difficult at times, of course, but I will explain in the chapter on leveling how one can go about setting such limits in a responsible way that is most apt to succeed.

I believe that young people, more than anything else, want freedom in this world, freedom of choice. What they do not understand is they must have the responsibility to go along with the choice. If you base your interaction with your children as they grow up on that premise, it will work out, because it says they earn the right to have the freedom and you will delegate it to them. If your child abuses that trust and responsibility, then you pull the chain in again. Unfortunately, there is a mentality in parenting that if you insist upon your children being responsible you are somehow taking away from their childhood. Who says you cannot have fun as a kid *and* be responsible for your butt?

The Rescue Triangle

Rescuing does not stop with children. We cover for adults who are in trouble; we try to patch up other's relationships when we don't like what is going on instead of letting them work it out themselves; we worry about what one friend thinks of another of our friends. Rescuing occurs in as simple a situation as writing a glowing letter of recommendation for an employee or a friend who you know for a fact has been performing poorly. In essence, when we rescue someone we are trying to be responsible for that other person's feelings and actions, and as we've already learned, that is impossible since only that person can be responsible for his or her own behavior.

An example of rescuing occurs in what is called the Rescue Triangle.

Notice from the direction of the arrows that people can switch roles, sometimes frequently, sometimes almost instantaneously. Parents will step in as rescuer when they see their child having difficulty accomplishing a task, such as tying a shoe. The child will often brush away their rescue with "I want to do it myself." (The shoe is playing the persecutor here). Feeling rejected, the parent becomes the victim, snapping at the child, "You don't appreciate anything I do, do you? I'm only trying to help you!"

The Rescue Triangle

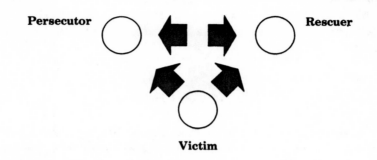

Persecutor   Rescuer

Victim

Or observe the following common scenario:

Young John is home from New York City, where he's been working in a large corporation since he graduated from college the year before. He's visiting mom and dad, and he tells dad the first day he's back, "Dad, I just made a big decision. I've invested in my first stock."

"Well, that's great son. What's the stock?"

"It's a new company called Signal Corporation. I've read the prospectus and I'm really excited about it, about developing my own portfolio."

"I'm real pleased. Where'd you get the money to invest? You haven't been working that long."

"I took all the money grandmother left me in her trust and invested it in this company."

"You did what!" John's father bolts from his chair. "You've pulled some dumb stunts in your time, boy, but this one takes the cake!"

At this point, dad has become the persecutor, his son the victim. The rescuer comes flying out of the kitchen, tea towel in hand.

"Big John, I don't think you need to talk to our son like that. He's a big boy now and he can make decisions for himself."

John Jr. turns to his mother and says, "Mom, can't dad and I ever have a man-to-man talk without you always interrupting?"

Now John Jr. has become the persecutor and his mother the victim.

"Don't you ever talk to your mother like that again! "Now Dad has become the rescuer.

This kind of role playing and role switching goes on all the time at all levels of society. We see it, for instance, in the popular hunger programs today. Donating food to the starving of Ethiopia is a form of rescuing. Now don't get me wrong. I'm not advocating we let people starve. A person on the edge of dying is not a person apt to be concerned about getting in touch with the fact they are 100 percent responsible for the mess they are in. We need to feed them; we also need to assist them to learn how to feed themselves, a more difficult yet more critical task. American politicians of all persuasions have recognized in the last few years that poverty programs too often perpetuate poverty because they reinforce rescuing.

Or take a situation where the word "rescue" is literally used: rescuing people trapped in a flood. How many times have we heard a flood victim, their house in the background floating out to sea, vow through gritted teeth that they intend to rebuild on the same damn spot? Do we rescue them again come the next flood? Provide them low-interest loans to rebuild in the same spot? Is that not rescuing that perpetuates the myth that others are responsible for our actions, that others will pick up the pieces?

Or take motorcyclists who ride without helmets or automobile passengers who travel without seat belts. They argue strongly for their freedom to go without helmets or seat belts, yet, when they are severely injured in an accident, they expect the rest of us to foot their medical expenses either through the insurance rates we all pay or the city-run hospital we fund through taxes. Perhaps they should be made aware of the consequences of their actions and their failure to take responsibility for themselves: no helmet or no seat belt, they foot the bill.

Rescuing is not limited to the poor or the "unfortunate. "We have in recent years rescued the Chrysler Corporation, shoe manufacturers, farmers, several city governments, banks, steel

179

companies, the federal government (each time we raise the debt ceiling) and just about anybody else with enough political clout and justifiable "excuses."

It is time to stop coming to the rescue of people every time they get themselves into a jam. According to the fundamental principles of total responsibility no one can be a victim . . . ever. Everybody is in the position they are in based on choice. That includes kids with bloated bellies in Ethiopia, battered wives (many battered wives continue to live in battering situations despite other options), and the homeless.

Say you know a friend who perpetually loses jobs or gets kicked out of his apartment because he never has enough money to pay the rent. Every three months he shows up on your door-step because he thinks he has no where else to go or any other options to follow. Predictably, he blames his situation on the economy or unfair employers or cheating landlords. Anybody but himself, right? And aren't friends people who mutually agree not to call each other on each other's stuff? So you rescue him, time after time.

Stop. You recognize you are totally responsible for your actions, and only your actions. So quit trying to be responsible for his actions too. Get him in touch with his own responsibilities by telling him that the next time he gets fired or thrown out onto the street he's going to have to find another solution to the problems he keeps creating. And stick to it when he comes banging on your door (he won't believe you that first time).

Cold-hearted? No. Are you risking the loss of a friend? Yes, he may never speak to you again except in epithets. But good friends are not rescuers.

This non-rescuing approach is one of the premises of a very controversial though successful organization called TOUGHLOVE. TOUGHLOVE was established to help parents who have lost disciplinary control of a child. An example of how TOUGHLOVE works is when a parent's child is arrested for possession of narcotics. This is a child who probably has been in trouble numerous times at school and with the law. The child calls his parents to bail him out. After all, they've done it before. But this time the parents refuse. Typically this shocks not only the child (the victim), but the police (the persecutors) as well. What parents would voluntarily leave their child in jail? TOUGHLOVE parents do because they recognize it is time to stop rescuing their child. As long as they keep bailing him out, getting charges reduced or dropped, covering up, they are keeping that child from learning to face the consequences of his actions. Rescuing him merely reinforces his belief that others are at fault (police, teachers, other kids) for whatever befalls him.

It is an anguishing step for parents to take. After all, most parents rescue their children from the time they are babies. They step into the squabbles with sister. They do their child's homework when he is late with his assignments. They pay for the toys she shoplifts. They cover his debts. It is difficult for us to stop rescuing people, but stop we must if we want to make total responsibility an effective principle instead of an empty value.

The greater the distrust (between people) the more difficult it is to level, but the need for leveling is that much greater.

—Robert Horton

16

"*Yeah, But . . .*"

One of the most powerful tools for efficient self-management, and for operating well in a world that basically does not understand self-management, is effective communication. It is difficult enough learning to play life from cause instead of effect without compounding the difficulty by "failing to communicate."

Yet people are incessantly complaining, "We aren't communicating." Companies have "poor communication" problems. Marriages crumble because husbands and wives "can't talk to each other." Parents complain that their kids don't make any sense.

One major reason we fail to communicate is because when most of us speak of "communicating" what we are doing, in reality, is attempting to get others to believe the way we believe. We're frustrated constantly with people we come into contact with because those people don't do what we would do if we were them.

As parents, our frustrations in "communicating" with our children come from our trying to get them to live up to the standards we think they ought to live up to because we have already been there. We want to save them from the errors of their ways. We make our bosses and our co-workers wrong. We get frustrated when they do not appreciate us or understand us. They are not open with us. We don't know what to do because when we sit down with them and begin to talk we think we are communicating, when in fact what we really are doing is trying to convince them to see things the way we see things, and vice versa. Both parties focus on the necessity of being right. When we deal with service people and repair people and sales people we get upset because they don't communicate with us the way we want them to. Their performance and standards and behavior do not meet our "high" standards.

But the problem in all these situations is not "poor communication." Poor communication is the symptom of the problem. What we really are saying is, "I do not *understand* things the way the other person understand things. I view things with a different set of values and priorities."

Much of our communication is an attempt to speak for others, to speak from *their* experience, not ours. "You are the one being irresponsible about this . . . You think I don't care, don't you! . . . Boy, did you screw that up . . . That's the dumbest thing you ever did . . . "

Yet we know if we accept the principles of total personal responsibility, it is impossible to speak to someone else's experiences. When we try, we are trying to drive that Circle of Responsibility backwards! We can only speak to *our* experiences and how we perceive that other person or set of events. It is the difference between saying, "You know I don't want to go" and "I don't want to go."

Effective communication stresses our acknowledgment that other people's experiences are uniquely theirs, and that their experiences and perceptions of those experiences may differ from ours. Effective communication is the ability of each person to express fully his or her own experiences, and for each person to listen to and understand the experiences of others. Effective communication, as opposed to ineffective, false, one-sided, or incomplete communication, allows people to be conscious of more alternatives on which to base their life choices.

What the real goal of effective communication ought to be then, is to establish effective, common *understanding*.

If you and I, as a relationship, understand each other, if I value the way you think and feel, and realize that the conditions of your experiences have been quite different from my experiences, and therefore you see things differently, I can enter a difficult situation understanding and respecting the differences we have. If, on the other hand, I enter that relationship convinced I'm absolutely right, and I want to convert you to the "right" way, then my goal of effective communication is doomed from the beginning.

You and I

As I suggested early in this chapter, communication often fails because we speak from "you" instead of "I." How many times have you had or heard the following conversations?

(Parent to teenager)
"No, you can't go to Florida for spring break."
"But Charlotte's getting to go. Why won't you let me go? I knew you'd say no. You never let me do anything!"
"You're too young and too irresponsible. No daughter of mine is going to be down there with all that booze and sex and drugs."

(Department chief to supervisor)
"Your report's worthless. This idea for reducing absenteeism is the stupidest thing I've ever seen."
"Yeah, but you're not the one who has to deal with these people every day."

(Wife to husband)
"God, you acted like a complete idiot at the party last night. If you wouldn't get so drunk, you—!"

"Oh, yeah! Well, you're just an old stick-in-the-mud."

When you start speaking from the other person's experience (using the word "you"), you are denying them the value of their experiences. You are pushing their buttons and launching your *Unc* Fighter. You are trying to make them wrong and you right.

In an organization or a marriage or any kind of relationship, such communication is disastrous. If managers belittle their employees, those employees are likely to become defensive, tentative, less cooperative, less enthusiastic, less creative, less productive. People will stop sharing ideas—the lifeblood of any organization. Instead of fostering growth and development, focusing on managing and planning, and stimulating creative solutions to problems, the organization will expend vast amounts of energy and time trying to resolve conflict, tension, interpersonal sideshows, and loss of productivity.

"I" statements express to the other person your belief in yourself, your confidence, your "perfectness." At the same time you are not putting them down nor being judgmental.

Let's play back those conversations approached from a position of responsible communication.

(Parent to teenager)

"No, I don't feel you should go to Florida for spring break. Why do you want to go?"

"Because all the kids I know are going. I think it'd be a lot of fun."

"It is. I went there myself a couple of times. My concern is that spring break is for college kids, not a sixteen-year-old. It can get pretty rough."

"I think I'm responsible enough to take care of myself."

"I think you are too. And I want you to go some spring. I simply feel this year isn't appropriate. What do you think if the family went to some place warm and sunny?"

(Department chief to supervisor)

"I'm not confident about this approach you've recommended for reducing absenteeism. Do you feel good about it?"

"Yes, I do. I came up with a lot of different approaches, and I think this one will work best."

"I appreciate your efforts, Donna. I still think this approach is unsatisfactory. You said you had some other ideas. I'd like to see what you think are your best three on my desk tomorrow."

(Spouse to spouse)

"I felt very upset last night, Alan. I thought your behavior was outrageous. I think you're drinking too much at these parties, and I'm not pleased about that."

"I understand your concern, Martha. And I don't think I drink excessively. I realize climbing onto their roof and baying at the moon might appear a bit bizarre, but there were seven other people up there with me."

What happened when we changed the "you's" to "I's"? We did not change anyone's opinions. The teenager still wants to go to spring break, the employee still believes she turned in a good report, and the couple still disagree about his behavior. What we have changed is the negation of each other, the trying to run the other person. In the case of the parent and the department chief, of course, they will have to make some final decision. But they did not put down the other person in the process. They did not try to make the other person "wrong." They left room for compromise. They upheld the other person's dignity and uniqueness.

When one realizes one cannot be inside another person, that what one sees is not what another person sees, then one begins to respect the quality of the other person *even though you may continue to disagree.* Using "I" instead of "you" forces you to *add to* the conversation instead of *arguing against it.* By conveying respect, even if you disagree, you will more likely receive respect back. Even in the situation of the teenager or the employee who must, in the end, accede to your decisions whether they agree or not (the employee can quit, of course), the fact you respected their viewpoints as uniquely theirs is more apt to engender better future relations and understanding. If you want your children or your employees or your friends or your co-workers to be more responsible for their own actions and attitudes, you must communicate your respect to them by concentrating on *understanding* their view of things.

Yeah, but . . .

"Yeah, but . . . " is a close kin to "you." Other variations are "well, but," "no, but," "sure, but," ad infinitum. In the supervisor-employee conversation the employee responded with a "yeah, but . . . " The use of the word "but" negates the other speaker's experience. It is a right-wrong approach. It launches *Unc* Fighters. It results in negative consequences. Listen to yourself for one day and notice how many conversations, including your own, are littered with "yeah, buts."

I prefer to eliminate the word "but" and substitute the word "and." Like the word "I," "and" *adds* to what other people say. When people say to me, "Ted, the idea that the people on KAL 007 chose to die is ridiculous," it's tempting to reply, "Yeah, but . . . " Instead, I say, "Thanks. I appreciate you sharing your thoughts. I can understand how you feel. It's a controversial concept and many people don't agree with it. In my experience, I think we all choose to . . . "

Meanwhile, the person who disagreed is chomping at the bit. Come on, Ted, fight.

Avoiding "you's" and "yeah, buts . . . " follows an old Zen principle called Tai Chi. Tai Chi is the principle of agreeing with someone's resistance. When you agree with someone's resistance, it forces them to take the energy they are expending on you and eat it. My wife Dorothy is excellent at doing this. I'm ranting and raving at her and she says, "I can tell you're upset, Ted, and you're *unc* and want to play *Unc* Fighter. Thanks for sharing that. I choose not to participate." I'm left there blowing air.

You can never play the game of right-wrong alone. Being in charge of your emotions is a powerful force. When you refuse to plug into the other person's baiting, it'll blow their socks off. They'd rather you wallow down there in the "Yeah, buts . . . "

On the Level

Consciously beginning to use "I" and "Yes, and" will go a long way toward developing effective understanding with other people. Basing your communications on *your experiences* is an excellent way to drive that Circle of Responsibility in the right direction. Another powerful tool in communicating your sense of personal responsibility is called leveling.

Leveling is the *responsible* communication of the truth as you

187

perceive it. Its intention is understanding. Leveling allows people to retain their credibility. It focuses on problems and difficulties with people's performance and behavior rather than on the people themselves. It focuses on opportunities for correcting problems and behavior. It entices suggestions, encourages ideas, stimulates imagination and creativity instead of defensiveness and narrow-mindedness. If done properly, leveling breaks down areas of distrust and builds areas of trust.

Dumping is the *irresponsible* communication of truth. It is dropping below the line on the ladder of the mind. Typically dumping begins with you . . . you . . . you. It is telling a colleague at work, "Can't you ever keep your mouth shut at these meetings!" Dumping occurs when your children ask you if there's a Santa Claus and you snap, "No, that's a stupid childish belief." Leveling is sitting down with them and explaining what you perceive as the spirit of Christmas, and then, if they ask you if there is a physical being that comes down the chimney and distributes gifts, you gently say no, but he is a spirit, a feeling that many of us believe in.

Dumping questions the quality of the person being dumped on. Its intention is to hurt feelings. "What do you think of my new dress?" "I wouldn't bury a dead cow in it."

Leveling is an art that takes practice and determination, but it can be one of the most effective and powerful communication tools you have. Here are suggestions to make leveling work for you.

Look to Self

To communicate effectively, the first thing we do, as we have so often in this book, is look to ourselves.

● **How tight are those artichoke leaves around you?**

You cannot level with someone, and you certainly cannot model the importance of open communication to others, if you've got those leaves wrapped tight around you. Peeling back those leaves is risky. You are making yourself vulnerable. But concealing the information blocks any potential for real communication. If the other person senses you are not being open, they are less likely to be open in return.

- ● **Clogged tubes impede communication.**

Lies keep you from being open with others. These are not only lies we make to ourselves (omission) or lies we make to others about ourselves (commission), but lies we make to others about them. Say you're angry about something your husband did, but you lie about how you feel because you're afraid of hurting his feelings. First, he is responsible for his feelings, not you. Secondly, you are depriving him of sincere feedback, which in the long term damages your relationship.

- ● **Effective communication is two-way.**

You not only express your thoughts and feelings, but you *listen* to the other person. You are conscious for them. You make good eye contact and convey your urgency in the matter. Poor understanding occurs frequently because one or both speakers are *unc* (see the chapter on Game playing). How many times have you found yourself in conversations in which your *yamma yamma* is going 90 miles an hour while the other person is speaking? You don't hear a single word because your *yamma yamma* is marshaling your response so the moment the other person pauses to take a breath you can cut in, believing what you have to say is much more important than what they have to say.

- ● **Examine the problem, not the person.**

Too often a parent will say to a child, "This room is a disaster. Can't you keep it cleaned up better than this?" Notice the parent is attacking the child, using the "you" and focusing on the problem. More effective communication is, "It's important to me this room be kept picked up. What do you think we can do to keep it clean?" Now the parent has conveyed his or her urgency about the situation and focused on the solution, not the child. The child is made to feel a part of the solution, not the cause of the problem.

- **Describe, don't evaluate.**

You are a supervisor at a corporation. Walter is an old and trusted employee, but lately he has failed to perform to your standards. A typical comment to Walter would be, "You've really disappointed me lately, Walter." Notice you've attacked Walter, not Walter's performance. Walter is likely to become defensive, feeling his self-esteem is being challenged. More productive is the approach of, "Walter, I've noticed lately that when I go by your office you often are not there. You've been late to meetings recently. You're dressing sloppily. Can you tell me how you see things? Do you see yourself doing these things? How do you view it?"

Now instead of targeting Walter you are examining Walter's actions. You are separating Walter the human being from the behavior Walter is displaying. You are not questioning his mother's sexual habits. You are conveying to Walter that you continue to love him as a fellow human being and the potential he has. Walter remains a perfect individual; indeed, he is probably still the dependable, trustworthy employee he has always been. But for reasons you as a supervisor do not yet know, aspects of his work behavior are not up to par. By examining Walter's behavior instead of Walter, you will decrease his defensiveness and increase the likelihood he will make the necessary changes.

- **Communicate love and respect.**

Most people, be they children, employees, or friends, desire respect, autonomy, recognition, and emotional security above money and power. Love and respect are not built on words but on actions. You must model it consistently at all times.

Leveling is difficult because people tend to take criticism as personal slander. How often have you heard your children say, in response to criticism of what they have done, "You don't love me. You hate me!"? Little Johnny slugs the kid next door and his parents come down on him with phrases like "Johnny, you're a bad boy," and "Billy won't like you anymore if you do that." Yet Johnny is not a bad boy. Johnny is a boy who has done a bad thing. His behavior is what is bad, not Johnny the person. Making that distinction is a critical difference between leveling and dumping.

● **Leveling should be based on specific examples.**

Before you sit down to level with someone, prepare notes. These notes should focus on specific incidents, specific things *you* have observed, not something someone else observed or told you they heard. And try to present your observations as soon as possible after the event. "Dear, I'm really unhappy about your behavior six months ago . . . " is not an effective approach.

● **Avoid good/bad.**

Don't make the person "wrong" and you "right." Too often communication is merely an attempt to play the right-wrong, win-lose, innocent-guilty game. People talk as if they are trying to score points in a Harvard-Yale philosophy debate. Winning becomes far more important than communicating.

● **Explore alternatives.**

Get the person involved in offering solutions. If Walter is arriving late to work, as a supervisor you must learn what the causes are and then ask him to suggest options to rectify the situation.

● **Provide useful information.**

Don't use leveling to let off personal steam. In effect, you are dumping when you throw a lot of garbage at someone just so you will feel better. The purpose of leveling is to provide useful observations to the other person, to work toward a mutual understanding of each other's perceptions of a situation.

- **Examine your own behavior.**

This gets back to the principle of the Circle of Responsibility. To level fully with someone else you must also open yourself up to examination. Even managers, from the company president down to a line supervisor, must be willing to listen to criticism from others as long as that criticism is also focused on behavior and not the individual.

A typical performance review of an employee is an excellent opportunity for the manager to say something like, "Now that we've reviewed your performance, Audrey, would you mind naming a couple of things you don't like about the way we work together."

"Well, you come on too strong at times. I think you're not as effective and efficient as you could be if you just backed off and relaxed a little more. I think I would respond to you better if you did."

"All right. Anything else?"

"One thing I've noticed is you seem to be impatient. You have good eye contact for a while, but then you look away and consequently I think you may not be home. Good eye contact is important to me."

Now the manager can take that information and agree or disagree with it, but either way the manager should not have any difficulty listening to the observations.

You Can't Hide

All communication is risky. Putting your ideas, thoughts, and feelings forward to others invites rejection—at the least of ideas, at the most of yourself. Insensitive, overbearing managers put down (or at worst, fire) employees who communicate information they do not want to hear; a spouse ridicules the other spouse;

parents belittle or ignore their children. Most of the world communicates from effect, which is why people hide behind safe rituals and games and withdrawal. But if you want to play life from cause instead of effect, if you want more choices in your life, you can't hide. If you are in an intolerable job situation, at what point does your mental health take precedent over the risks? At what point does your happiness take precedent over what you perceive as inconsiderations of a spouse? At what point does the desire for a strong relationship with your children overcome the uncertainties you have about trying to communicate with them? Avoiding the "You's" and "Yeah, buts . . . ," and communicating through leveling what you perceive as the truth may be risky. But not communicating is the greater risk.

Your responsibility out there is to cause something to happen, not wait for something to happen.

—Bear Bryant

17

Five Steps to Effective Communication

I'm going to ask you to take a risk. I'm going to ask you to set up a one-hour leveling session with someone with whom you have urgently wanted to communicate. It may be your boss, your spouse, your teenage child, a friend, a parent. It may be more than one person; it may be about more than one issue, though my suggestion is to initially focus on one person and one issue. A leveling session the first time around is a powerful experience. Move on to other issues and other people after you do the first one and you can review the results.

A leveling session comprises five major ingredients:

1. Take charge of the situation.

You must go from being *unc* and emotionally controlled to having your mind and body at home at the same time. You should try to be composed (breath deeply to relax yourself). Think about what you want to say. Write it out beforehand if necessary. You then must communicate that you want to resolve the issue.

"There's an issue I'm having some concerns about, some frustrations I'm experiencing, and I'd like to kick it around with you. Can I sit down with you and have, say, an hour of uninterrupted time to discuss the problem?"

Notice you are talking from your experience here. You don't walk in and say "You're making me mad . . . You're upsetting me . . . You're late . . . You're out of control . . . You're driving me crazy . . . "

The first time or two you do this will probably put your spouse or your kids or your employees or boss in a state of shock. Once they recover, you can arrange the leveling session, either beginning at that moment, or later at a mutually convenient time. A quiet, comfortable place, and uninterrupted time are crucial.

2. Outline your experience.

Start the leveling session by outlining, *from your experience,* what you see as the problem. "Look, I'm frustrated and this is what I see happening." Use phrases like "I think . . . I have observed . . . I have experienced . . . I feel . . . I believe. Avoid the "you" statements. This is the heart of the leveling process: communicating the truth responsibly as you perceive it. Follow the leveling techniques described in the last chapter.

3. Ask the other person's experience.

You need to be quiet long enough and listen well enough (slow down that *yamma yamma,* don't debate, don't say, "Yeah, but . . . ") to have them tell you how *they* view the situation. Just as we all have a different view of an accident, we all have different experiences and different views of every interaction and event in our life. Give the other person a few minutes to express his or her experience (one hopes from an "I" viewpoint).

4. Correct the problem.

Once the person has expressed his or her views, which may differ markedly from yours, then ask, "What are we going to do to correct the problem?" We have decided we are going to do this and this and this. We are going to come to each other when such and such occurs. We are not going to behave as we have before. Whatever the solution, summarize exactly what behavior each of you has agreed to change or adopt.

Ideally, a leveling session reaches a win-win conclusion, in which the course of action is *mutually* beneficial to both parties. A leveling session should never be used to play right-wrong, win-lose. There are occasions, as we will see, where at best a leveling session clarifies understandings, but does not result in actions both parties are completely pleased about.

5. Secure follow-up support.

The last but nonetheless critical step: To make certain the agreed-upon changes are carried out, you need to schedule one or more follow-up meetings to review how you've been doing since the leveling session. It may be two or three days later, a week, or whatever length seems appropriate. Sit down and say, "Remember the conflict we had last week? I need to take some time to make sure we're where we said we were going to be." Don't go too long before having a follow-up session, or you will lose the momentum and energy sparked at the original session.

Many times at the follow-up session you will mutually agree that the issue has been resolved or at least improved. But sometimes it isn't. One or both of you will end up saying, "Well, you're still doing the same damn thing" and the other will say, "Well, I don't care and I'm *not going to change*." Even if this occurs, at least you are making an effort. I think you will find it a lot tougher to continue doing that same piece of behavior when you've talked about it, even though you want to be right.

This leveling process is a way to reclarify the rules of the game and reclarify the behavior expected of us. Leveling provides the support mechanism and the caring necessary to improve it.

Leveling needs to happen all the time. It should happen any time you want to clear the air. It should take place any time you want to reaffirm the rules of the game. "Let's sit down and talk. Can we take an hour out? Can we level with each other?"

Most of us do not do that because we are so preoccupied emotionally and locked into our schedules and priorities. We are not conscious much of the time. If you're like me, usually what happens is I yell and scream or do something that says "I want your behavior to start changing," and usually my wife or my children continue to do exactly what they want to do because they like seeing me ticked off. Children will play "let's-get-daddy's goat" just out of sheer boredom.

Examples

You may still be wary of this whole process of leveling. It is risky. So let's run through a couple of typical leveling scenarios, one with a teenage daughter and one with a boss.

As in the past, parents these days often talk about not being able to communicate with their children. I am a parent of two teenagers who go to clone school (you know it's clone school because you can drop them off there in the morning and pick up anybody else's at night and it won't make any difference), who look to the sky in disgust when we ask such profound questions as "Good morning, how are you?," and who change radio stations as fast as possible. I know from experience how difficult it is when children do not see things the way we would like them to. Why? Because most of us feel they were placed on this planet to live up to our expectations. The notion that they are here to live up to their own expectations is as remote as the moon to most of us. So I may set up a leveling session just to clear the air.

Sometimes they are frustrated with me about something. In our family, any member can ask for a leveling session with any other member. Leveling is never a one-way street: parent to child or boss to employee. Not only is it the fair thing to do, it gets back to modeling again. If you expect them to listen to you in a leveling session, to listen to your gripes, then you must be willing to listen to them. Unfortunately, too often the following scenario occurs instead.

"Why can't I stay out later, Dad? All my friends get to. It's not fair having to be in by eleven. You're treating me like a little girl!"

To which Dad typically replies, "I don't give a damn what you say. When I was your age I never stayed out past eleven. I never even had a car. So forget it. You ain't doing it." That is called dumping. It usually ends up in yelling and playing old tapes from prior conflicts.

At our house, dumping is not allowed. My daughter Megan might say to me, "Dad, I want to talk about my weekend curfew. I'm seventeen years old. I think my twelve o'clock curfew is too early. I think I've shown through my grades and the way I've handled myself and my driving ability, and the way I've contributed to the family, that I ought to be given a one o'clock curfew on weekends."

Notice Megan (1) has taken charge of the situation by asking for the meeting and (2) summarized her concerns and her justification for a change based on her view that she is grown up and deserves more responsibility.

Then I must express my experience of the situation. (3) I may tell Megan I'm afraid something is going to happen to her, because I've been around for 40-odd years, and I would like her to make the best possible decision at 17 with my years of experience, and that's not going to happen.

We may compromise (4). We may agree to 12:30 instead of 1:00. If I see certain other changes in her behavior I might allow her to stay out later. Or I might not agree to the change at all, or I might be more open to her request after the next report card. I also might say I need to digest that information, I want to talk it over with her mom, and we'll provide an answer the next day.

Megan then provides a conclusion (5), a follow-up. "Okay, Dad, it's my understanding we're going to continue to talk about it and monitor how well I do in school the next two months. If I do well, you're going to extend my curfew hours. In the meantime, I want to be able to talk to you again about the situation." Fine, I reply.

As a parent you have established for your children—consistently and fairly, one hopes—rules of the game for living with you. As a parent you will listen to what your child asks, but this does not mean you will agree with everything. This is one of those examples we discussed earlier, in which I felt I had a responsibility as a parent to make certain decisions. One value of a leveling session is it usually forces the parent to ask, Is my child (you can substitute employee or friend or spouse) asking to do something I do not think is responsible for me as a parent to let the child do? Or is my child asking me to do something I would not do if it were I? Leveling allows you to consider these questions in a rational, calm atmosphere; dumping will force all issues into the first category. If your answer to the first is yes, you have a responsibility to say, "I understand what you have to say. I appreciate your request. And I don't feel it's responsible for me as a parent to allow that to happen at this time. I want to make sure you understand. You may not agree, but it's important you understand." If, upon reflection during the leveling session, your answer is the second category, explain the potential consequences to the child and let him or her go at it.

It is important even if you decide you will not alter the arrangement (no, you must still come in by midnight), that you encourage your child to continue to take the risk and energy to request future alterations in the rules.

Leveling is the responsible communication of the truth. The real purpose of holding these leveling sessions is not always to agree, but to make certain we "understand" each other. Many times in my household we do not agree, but we do have a high understanding of each other because of these leveling sessions. Such understanding is vital to the deepening of our relationship and the conveying of the urgency of being responsible for one's self. How many parents do you know who effectively communicate with their kids?

In this particular example, Megan did not get what she wanted: to stay out until 1:00 a.m. However, she did get a clarification of the rules in a responsible, non-argumentative atmosphere. This alone is important, for young people want consistency. They do not want us to ask any more of them than we are willing to give. The old idea that we can do anything we want to because we are the boss doesn't work anymore because kids ask why—and they deserve to. Furthermore, she also was able to lobby for a potential change in the future. If she had chosen to dump on me instead of leveling, the words would have flown like cat fur and she would not have gained anything.

On The Job

We encounter similar needs to level on the job, with fellow employees, bosses, and subordinates. I talk to company employees nearly every day. I constantly hear comments such as "He doesn't appreciate me, she doesn't understand me, he won't delegate to me, I don't have enough authority, I don't know what I am doing, there's poor communication, there's duplication of effort . . . "

What that means is from our perception many of us have a poor understanding of what is going on at work, and other people at the company do not understand things the way we do. If you are truly interested in improving the communication (understanding) between yourself and those you work with, if you feel a lack of understanding is hampering your effectiveness and productivity, or making your job hell, then you have a definite responsibility to level with the appropriate people. You do not have a right to bitch and moan and make excuses.

Let's say you work for a person under whom you are not exactly sure what your responsibilities are. Priorities and authority seem vague, subject to frequent change. You find yourself spinning your wheels, frustrated. If you are genuinely interested in clarifying the situation and obtaining specific changes, I strongly recommend you ask for a one-hour leveling session with your boss. The purpose of this meeting, in your mind, is to clarify the priorities in your job, and the boss's view of your authority.

The thought of "leveling" with the boss strikes terror in the hearts of many. "My god, I could lose my job over this . . . He'll kick me down to the warehouse . . . She'll see I never work in this town again!" Yes, there is risk. However, I suggest that if you handle the leveling session professionally and with respect (avoiding those "you" statements, etc.), you may in fact raise your status with the boss, especially if you are one of several employees under the person. By leveling, you are showing your professionalism and your dedication to your job. For leveling in effect says, I am concerned about how well I do my job and I think if we clarify the rules of the game I can do a better job for you and the company. Not many bosses will argue with that reasoning. Yes, some will see any attempt at leveling as a challenge to their authority or a nuisance. You know best how your boss is likely to react, though in fact your boss may react more openly to this than you initially fear, especially if your request for a leveling session is well handled.

As in the case of parent and child, leveling with your boss involves five steps:

1. Boss, I would like to sit down with you and kick some things around. I need one hour, uninterrupted, for us to sit and talk. To which your boss is likely to respond, what are you talking about? Well, I think sometimes your understanding of what my responsibilities and authorities are and my understanding are two different sets of understanding. I want to make sure we have the same understanding so I can work most effectively and productively (notice I am taking charge.)

   Okay, the boss agrees. You offer to come early or stay late—whatever you need to do to get that hour. There should not be anyone in any organization who cannot manage to get one hour, uninterrupted, with their boss—not if it is important enough to you.

   But my boss won't listen or she won't take the time, you argue. If your boss refuses to meet with you (I don't want to, don't bug me, I haven't got the time), say you understand, but persist nonetheless. You must convey the urgency of leveling. Don't say, "Sometime when you have a moment, boss," or "That's okay, there's no rush." Do that and your boss will stall forever. Your very demeanor must convey urgency. Maintain eye contact. Don't scream or rant and rave; do be persistent.

   If your boss continues to refuse, say fine, I'll be making an appointment with your superior next week. I'll let you know when the meeting is, and we'd both love to have you there. Always go through the chain of command, never around. If you go to your boss's superior, the superior will, if he or she does not want to model rescue, ask if you have talked to your boss already, and if not, you'll get kicked back to your boss anyway.

Scary? Hell, yes! You could go right through the chain of command and right out the company doors. But how badly do you want to correct the situation? Are you miserable in your job because of what you perceive are intolerable demands or conditions imposed from above, too many duties and not enough authority, too much political infighting or office tensions? Then understand that if you are not willing to take the responsibility to fix the situation you have no right to bitch. You are part of the problem if you do not cause something to happen. You are 100 percent responsible for everything that happens to you in your life. You either produce excuses or you produce results. Leveling is a very effective way to produce results.

2.   You've taken charge and you've arranged the meeting. Now you sit down with your boss, in either the boss's office, yours, or in a quiet, neutral corner. Whatever seems comfortable. Be in command from the beginning. Maintain eye contact. Bring a note pad with the principal points you want to make. If this is a leveling session to clarify your responsibilities and authorities (not all leveling sessions have to be about traumatic issues), bring along what is fondly called a job description sheet, or be prepared to write one for yourself during the session.

"John, the reason I asked for the meeting is that I made a commitment to myself to spend some time to go through some things with you I think are in the best interest of the company and our working relationship. I seem to spend a lot of time spinning my wheels. I think that's because when I'm working with people, I don't always *understand* what things I'm responsible for, the priorities, the way they need to be done. I want to clarify those things with you."

You then proceed through the job description. Typically, if you are in a managerial position those responsibilities include:

"Maintain. . . . . . .
"Establish. . . .
"Coordinate . . .
"Hire and fire. . . .
"Ensure inventory controls . . .
"Generate status reports every two weeks. . . .
"Initiate. . . .
"Ensure that capital expenditures. . . .
"And all the crap not covered above . . ."

3.   Review the list item by item. Make certain your understanding of your responsibilities and your boss's understanding of your responsibilities match. This may seem like a
rudimentary exercise, but you'd be surprised how often you
discover that expectations don't match, or responsibilities are
falling through the cracks, or responsibilities have changed.
Clarify the priorities (often an area of confusion).

Go through the list again to determine precisely how
much authority you have for each item: do you have complete
authority, should you act and then report, or must you obtain approval? Take as much authority as you can for each
item. There may be some give and take. If you do not have
the authority you think you need, make that clear to your
boss.

Clarify the top priorities: bosses and employees frequently
differ in perception here.

4.   Correct any problems that have become evident during the
leveling session. Try to mutually agree on solutions. Of
course, you may have differences with your boss, and at some
point the boss is going to say "This is the way it will be."
Fine. You've had your say. If you still don't like the rules of
the game, try again later (not behind the boss's back) to
change them. Like Megan, try to establish conditions and
goals you can meet that might motivate change. If you still
can't live with the rules, go play another game somewhere
else. Even if no major changes are made, the session remains

valuable because it strengthens understanding between each of you. People who know and understand each other more clearly are people who live and work together more effectively, even if they do not agree on every point.

5.   Follow-up may consist of arranging another meeting in two weeks or thirty days to see how things are working. Does your list of responsibilities and authorities fit the realities of the job? You may feel you are off target from your last leveling session and you want to have another one. Do the follow-up as long and as often as necessary to get the problems corrected. The important point is to keep working at your understanding of the rules of the game.

At this point there should be absolutely no misunderstandings. If there was bullshit going on before, you should have cut through it. You may work in a firm of only a few employees, where conditions are much more informal. There may be no written job description. You may not have 15 duties or you may not be a manager. Nonetheless, the leveling still can be useful, if for nothing else than establishing better rapport and mutual respect and cooperation. If and when problems should arise, you've already established a good foundation on which to iron out those problems.

If you work in a job in which you are a supervisor or manager, I would suggest you conduct the same leveling session with the employees directly under you (which should not be more than eight or ten). If all of them have identical duties, you can consider a group leveling session, but I think individual sessions are more effective. Your approach is the same as with your boss. Explain that you want to meet for an hour to clarify the employee's responsibilities and authority. Or perhaps you have a specific concern about the employee: absenteeism, lateness, poor productivity, feuding with fellow employees.

Whatever the reason for the meeting, make certain the session is *uninterrupted*. Don't say, "Excuse me," when the phone rings or someone knocks on your door. You cannot model urgency to the employee if you do not treat it with urgency. Convey your perceptions. Listen to your employee. You may learn of information that will change your perception. There may be give and take. More likely, if you are discussing a problem, you'll hear excuses. Don't make the employee wrong for making the excuses. The employee is probably coming from effect to begin with. Instead, try an approach such as, "What other choices do you have?" This not only reduces defensiveness, it puts the employee in a position of thinking for himself, of forcing him to be pro-active.

There may be issues where you as boss must say, "I disagree with your perceptions of the issue and this is the way it will be." But at least you have given the employee fair hearing, and you have communicated your resoluteness on the matter clearly and with urgency, something that many organizations do not do with their employees. Understanding and expectations will not be the issue. If the employee continues to be late or absent or inefficient, then that employee will be history.

Again, you may think such a session is unnecessary, but who ends up suffering the consequences when your employees fail to carry through with assignments?

The same kind of leveling is valuable between co-workers: business partners, managers with departments that work together, fellow supervisors, employees you work with every day. Obviously you may not need an hour leveling session with a co-worker. Perhaps you've had a minor conflict of duties with another worker. Ten or fifteen minutes are all you may need. The important points are conveying the urgency, communicating in the "I," and following the five steps to effective communication.

1. Take charge of the situation.
2. Outline your experience.
3. Ask the other person's experience.
4. Correct the problem.
5. Secure follow-up support.

The object is to define the rules of the game.

Leveling carried on in any corporation, large and small, can be one of the most dynamic tools a company can employ. Poor understanding is the root of many company problems, from poor job performance to lack of creativity and enthusiasm. So often new people are hired, plunked into a job, handed a printed job description (and not always that), and expected to figure out the rest. They have virtually no sense of what drives that particular company—that is, what is its "corporate culture." Consequently, the new employee screws up and the company does not understand that the employee's understanding of the culture and the company's understanding are two different understandings. Alienation is the result.

Management is not that tough. It is common sense. Unfortunately, we use little common sense when we employee people. How can a company expect its employees to know what it is thinking if no one tells them anything? Countless studies have shown that what is more important to employees than money is good working conditions, job satisfaction, feeling appreciated, feeling "in" on things. Leveling helps achieve that. Leveling means a heightened sense of urgency, more eye contact, greater consciousness, a caring and respect for each other. It instills teamwork, company spirit, people working with instead of for each other, and most of all, greater individual responsibility and modeling of that responsibility.

The Rest of the World

Besides home and on the job, leveling can be used every day in our interactions with people in our world—restauranteurs, car mechanics, sales clerks, real estate agents, the telephone company. Usually situations with them are triggered by disappointment. The other person is not or will not do things the way we want them done. The tendency is for us to plug into upset.

Now obviously you are not likely to have a one-hour, uninterrupted, sit-down session with your car mechanic. But you can run through the same five steps. Imagine yourself talking to the service manager at a car dealership.

First, get the manager conscious as to the urgency you feel about the problem. "We're leaving on vacation in one week and we need to have a new catalytic converter installed before we go. No excuses. It's got to be on and working before we go." Don't be vicious or yell or cuss, but do be firm. Establish good eye contact. Convey that urgency.

"I want to work with you, Al, but I'm concerned about the dollar amount I'm going to be spending, and I'm extremely concerned about the time you may have the car. I've had people at other places promise me all kinds of things and then never deliver. What can I do to make sure there aren't going to be any problems? Is there any reason for me to be concerned? As I said, my family and I are leaving in one week and I don't want any delays. Are you sure you can get the part in time? Can I talk directly to your parts manager? Can I check with you later on precisely what's being done?"

Notice that at this point you have separated yourself from 99 percent of the population, because most people do not do this. Most people "assume" that when they hand their car keys to the manager that matters are well in hand. They never question that there might be a problem. They never question that the part they need might be in another state, subject to shippage delays. They're going to let the manager pack their parachute for them, and then bitch when it doesn't open.

You, on the other hand, have got this service manager's attention. You've got him thinking you better not be taken lightly (there's that reflection again), that you will go to the president of the dealership to make sure things are done right. Plus, the sales manager will probably recognize that if they do a good job you're the kind of person who will tell that to other people.

Take yourself out of the ordinary. *Cause* things to happen. Do it in a responsible manner. Don't let others control you, don't rise to the bait if they get angry or upset.

Leveling can be scary at first, but if you begin to apply it to all aspects of your life you will find yourself more effectively taking control of your life, of getting those around you to begin to operate from cause instead of effect. The choices you'll be making will be choices you want instead of merely the choices you've allowed others to make for you.

Can two walk together, except they be agreed?
—The Bible

18

Agreeing to Agree

At the conclusion of many leveling sessions, and frequently in less formal situations, is a sixth step: the parties involved come to an *agreement*. Whether it is to agree on what the budget will be for the coming year or to agree with a friend to meet for lunch two days from now or to agree with your daughter on when she must be home at night, an agreement involves each party producing results.

Let's go back to that leveling session with your boss. At the end of the session you should say something similar to the following: "Martha, as I see it, we have a complete understanding about my responsibilities and your responsibilities, and I have a clear understanding of my authority level for each one of my jobs. We have come to a common understanding on the priorities of the job. Should there be any variations in that, I have a responsibility to come back to ask for another leveling session. Now I want to establish an agreement that you will produce as agreed and that I will produce as agreed. Do we have an agreement?"

Before Martha and you answer that, let's establish what exactly is an agreement. Poll any number of people and they're likely to tell you that an agreement is:

a commitment
a contract
an understanding
a promise
a pact
an arrangement
a pledge
a guarantee

Certainly an agreement contains those elements. But what about YOUR WORD! Whatever happened to the notion that "a person is only as good as *his or her word*"? Remember when a handshake meant something? What happened to it? Why do we need to bring in a raft of lawyers and accountants to strike even the simplest of agreements? (We bring them in later to find loopholes to get out of the agreement.)

Why doesn't anyone trust anyone anymore? Trust once related to dependability, to accountability, to ensuring that someone else would look out for our best interests because people treated people the way they wanted to be treated. We still have the same definition of trust, but I think people are more interested in themselves at the expense of other people. I think we talk a good game, but we don't model keeping agreements. That is an underlying fundamental value we have missed in the element of total responsibility. We don't have the same sense of urgency, the same sense of passion about agreements.

In my world of total responsibility, once an agreement is established, that's it. Once I give you my word, that's it! Once you give me your word, that's it! There are no excuses for not producing the results agreed to. No exceptions, no alterations (one can make changes if both parties concur, which I'll discuss later). No,"I'm sorrys." No, "Yeah, but I was only a few minutes late." You do it or you don't. When one makes an agreement, one does not *try* to keep one's word—trying is shoveling.

A person who keeps agreements, without fail and without excuses, is a person living total responsibility. It is a stamp of recognition that this person operates life from cause, that this person is not going to find fault or blame others. What other kind of person would you possibly want to deal with?

An agreement requires a clear, *conscious* awareness of the commitment necessary to get common understanding, and results will be achieved without excuses. The power of making agreements is it compels individuals to do exactly what they say they are going to do. It fosters clarity, precise action, anticipation, creativity, effectiveness, productivity. It eliminates such daily nonsensical communication as "Hihowareyoufinehavelunchsure."

My language for an agreement may not be yours. It does not

210

even have to be verbal, especially with people you know well. But it must be conveyed and understood, and *understood* that it is understood. Why this apparent extra formality? Without this final step, without this formal closure of a transaction between individuals (or companies or governments), one cannot convey the urgency and the commitment of that agreement. No significant change in the attitude and actions of individuals can occur. Too often we agree to something without that sense of urgency and commitment. We don't stop to think, "I need to take 100 percent responsibility. Am I willing to do everything necessary to get this thing done that I have agreed to?" Upon reflection, if you think you cannot keep the agreement, don't make it.

This formal closure is especially important with people who play from effect instead of cause. How many times have you asked someone, Will you do this for me, and they've replied, already halfway to the door, "Yeah, yeah, I'll get it for you." You know right then they are only half listening, that they are not home, that you'd have better odds playing the craps tables in Vegas than betting they are going to do what they just agreed to do. So why do that to yourself! What you need to say is, Excuse me, will you come here for a moment. Would you mind telling me what you just agreed to do for me?

Remember the salesman for my seminar manuals? I made absolutely certain he understood exactly what I wanted and when I wanted it. I made eye contact with him, I made sure he was conscious for me and I was conscious for him. There could be no trying on his part. He produced the results he agreed to or he paid through the nose for failing. Do we have an agreement?

Agreements are one of the most powerful ways to drive the Circle of Responsibility in the proper direction. To rebuild our world of shattered integrity, to rebuild trust among us, people must make fewer agreements than they have been making—but keep a lot more of the ones they do make.

Agreement Defined

For an agreement to take place between two or more people, there first must be an "intention"—that energy that precedes the process of deciding—and the agreement must produce a mutually beneficial result. Both parties must conclude and accept that the terms of the agreement are acceptable and beneficial to both.

Agreement

Reflection of One Another

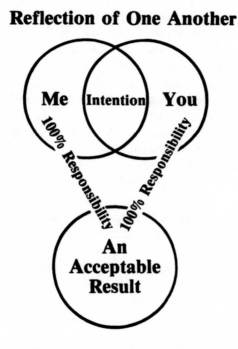

Orders are not agreements ("Take that hill!"). All orders supersede agreements. The fact is, however, most transactions in our personal and professional life are agreements. We agree to produce a report by a certain time, we agree to take our children to the circus, we agree to meet a friend for lunch, we agree to carry out a task for our mate. Unfortunately, life's transactions are all too frequently broken. In a world playing from effect, who needs to keep agreements. It's fashionable to be late. It's somebody else's fault, right? Or worse, people just don't give a damn. Recall the many times in your life when someone failed to carry out a task the two of you had agreed to. I don't mean just professionally. I'm talking about children who didn't clean up their room, friends who said they were coming to your party but didn't, mechanics who said they would have your car fixed by tomorrow but didn't, babysitters who canceled at the last moment. This is to say nothing of broken political agreements and social agreements. (People who break political agreements or societal agreements have grown up watching the toleration of broken "minor" agreements.)

There are no excuses . . . ever!

In the world of 100 percent personal responsibility, you either produce the results on time, as agreed, or you produce the excuse of why you haven't. No "I'm sorrys" or "Yeah, buts . . . " or "I tried." You step in it or you don't.

Having It Both Ways

Someone makes an agreement with you. You want them to keep it, right? Are there exceptions? How often? All the time? Who decides? I make an agreement with you to appear at a seminar you have arranged. The day before the seminar is to begin it snows heavily and the airport is closed. To you it is important the seminar be held as arranged, for a later time will not work. You've gone to trouble and expense to have your employees there. Is it okay if you and your people show up but I don't?

Of course not!

So why do we treat our own agreements so cavalierly? How many times have we been late to something and dismissed it, or blamed it on the traffic? Don't we tend to down play our failure to keep our agreement? But notice what happens in reverse.

When someone else fails to keep their commitment with you, aren't you irritated, if not downright furious?

According to our principle of reflection, what is the only way to feel justified in expecting others to keep their word with you? When you do not keep your word, how can you expect other people to keep theirs? Yet too often agreements are made this way: I want you to keep your word with me all the time, without fail. Oh, by the way, I'll do my best; if I don't, I want you to know that I tried. Or, please know that something came up.

We frequently do this with our children. We expect them, we tell them, to keep their word with us, yet because we are the "parents," because we are in charge and we have so many weighty "responsibilities" in life, we don't think twice about breaking our word to them. "I know I promised to take you to the movie, but something came up at work and I can't." We rationalize this by saying the "something at work" is more "important" than our commitment to our children. We know what are the greater priorities in life. How many people have the guts to tell their boss, "No, I can't come in Saturday afternoon to do the report because I've already promised to take my children to a movie"?

But Ted, if I don't go in I may risk losing my job. It's not fair to my children to risk my job just to go to a movie with them. They'll understand—at least when they are older.

This, of course, is how we teach our children, through modeling, to break agreements, to accept the fact that others will break agreements (hence, to use as an excuse for what happens to us).

But Ted, my job—

To begin with, I doubt that rarely a job or even a promotion is on the line. We cave into those last-minute requests because we feel it is more important to appease the boss than keep agreements with our children. Second, there often are other options, such as working at other times to finish the report. Third, never make a commitment to your children in the first place if there is any doubt you can fulfill that agreement. You do not have to make agreements; you only have to keep the ones you do make. The fact is, most reports don't pop up at the last minute—not if you are being anticipatory. You need to take the steps to ensure the report is finished before Saturday. Fourth, if you have consis-

214

tently kept your word in the past at work, if your boss understands your urgency about commitments, the boss is more apt to be flexible and understanding when you explain you have made a prior commitment to your children.

Altering Agreements

I am not saying that once an agreement is made it is carved in stone. You can alter agreements—if *both* parties agree to the change and the change is made *prior* to the agreed-upon time. If a real emergency arises, ask your children if you can alter the agreement. See if there is not an alternate time you can attend the movie. Most people recognize legitimate emergencies and are more than willing to reschedule. And if you do screw up—and we all do—acknowledge it and move on.

It is the excuse-making after the fact that must not be tolerated. When people say they can't keep their agreements, they are saying they choose not to. To me, there is a big difference between sauntering in ten minutes late for an appointment, excuse or no excuse, and calling ahead to say, "Ted, something's come up. Will it be okay with you if we meet at 10:15 instead of 10:00?" This is not merely a courtesy, but a specific request to alter a prior agreement. "That's fine, Alice. We'll meet at 10:15."

Of course, if at 10:15 I have a prior meeting with someone else, I'm going to tell Alice, "No, that is not a good time." I then have two choices. I can tell Alice we'll simply meet on another day, or, if the meeting with Alice was to provide, say, information I needed for the 10:15 appointment I would tell Alice she better get herself to my office by 10:00. She made an agreement, and she cannot arbitrarily and single-handedly alter that agreement.

Holding to this line can be painful (so what else is new in life). You've made an 11:30 luncheon date with a business associate to discuss an important matter. At 11:00 Stephanie, an old friend, calls from the airport. She's got a three-hour layover on a flight to St. Louis and she wants to have lunch. You explain to Stephanie you have a previous commitment but you will call to see if you can alter it. You call your business associate and ask to alter the agreement. You do not call and say "Something came up, Jim, and I'll catch you later." (How many times have you had that said to you?). Now Jim may be perfectly agreeable to changing to a later luncheon date, especially if you explain the circumstances to him. However, if he says, "No, we really need to meet today," you will have to call Stephanie back and say, "I can't, I've got a previous commitment. How are things going?"

Now this may seem unfair and rude to Stephanie; but if Stephanie is an old friend who knows *from experience* (that modeling again) that you are a person who keeps your agreements, she will understand.

Another example:You are in charge of a meeting scheduled from 9:00 to 10:00. At 9:55 you say, "We have two more items to discuss and we need another half hour. Can all of you stay until 10:30?" Everyone says yes except for one person who has a prior commitment at 10:15. "Okay. We'll reschedule the items. Meeting adjourned."

I learned the importance of keeping agreements the hard way. In 1976, when I started my company, I contracted in August with a real estate firm to do my seminar on November 4, 5, and 6. My procedure at the time was to bill clients for my fee and the cost of the program at the end of the conference. In September I received a call from a large chemical company in Michigan wanting me to speak before their annual convention on November 6. I explained that I had a prior commitment but could they change the date I could speak? No, they could not. I called the real estate firm and asked if we could change the seminar dates. No, that was the only time they could do it. I swallowed the fact that I was a struggling young company and called the chemical company to say they would have to get someone else. Two days before the real estate program, the firm's president called to say he had just sold the firm to another corporation and they were canceling the seminar.

I remember sitting in my office that day wondering why I had chosen to do that to me (well, not exactly in those words).

216

Shortly thereafter, I established a policy requiring all seminar programs to be booked and paid for *several months* in advance. No money, no agreement. Of course, I was told that no new company could do such a thing. You wanna bet! Since then I have never had a company cancel and I have never had anyone complain about paying in advance.

In turn, I make an agreement to *never* miss a program or be late (and I never have, though I have flown to the other end of the country as much as two days early to ensure that), and I guarantee the quality of my seminars, money back if you don't like it. Since 1976 I can count on one hand the number of *individuals* who have requested their money back.

What if you get sick, Ted, or worse, choose an airplane that crashes? Now why would I choose to get sick or die if I have an agreement to do a program?

Ask yourself this. Among your friends and acquaintances, among the vendors and supervisors you work with, among the service people you deal with for your car and your home, do not the ones who keep their word stand out? Who do what they say they will do? Aren't they the people you go back to time and time again, or enjoy working with or being with the most?

And if you are not experiencing much agreement-keeping in your life, have you looked at how well you are keeping the agreements you make? What incentive do friends have to show up on time for dinner at your house if you are consistently late to theirs?

While I personally am more hard-nosed about agreements than most people, it does not mean I am not flexible. I am always open to changing agreements if it is reasonable, though someone who is constantly requesting alterations becomes suspect after a while.

The same goes for broken agreements. I recognize that none of us is 100 percent perfect in our behavior. We all make mistakes, we all fall off the bicycle now and then. If someone is late one time for lunch with me, it doesn't mean I'm going to stick them on my Never Again list. At the same time, there are only so many broken agreements I am going to experience with that person before I choose not to make an agreement again with them. There is no magic number, of course. Each of you must decide for yourself how many broken agreements you are willing to put up with. They are your choices, you know. I guarantee, however, that you—and the people you know and meet in life—will find that the more personally responsible you become the less indulgent you will be in experiencing other people's broken promises.

Ask my kids about this. When my kids make agreements with me they keep them, because they know if they don't they'll be staring at the ceiling of their room for the next month. In my world there is only one clock, and it is mine. I've watched Scott race across our backyard at 4:59 and slide into the kitchen yelling "Safe!"

One evening a friend called Megan to see if she wanted to go to a local shopping mall. Kids love to hang out at malls; they never buy anything but they love to hang out there. She asked me if she could go and I said, yes, but you have to be home by 10:00. She told her friend it's okay, but she has to be back by 10:00. Her friend says her older sister is driving and sure, they can be home around 10:00. No, you don't understand, says Megan. I gave my dad my word I would be home by 10:00, and not one minute later. Megan then talks to her friend's older sister, but she remains unconvinced in her own mind that she could guarantee that she could get home by 10:00. She chose to stay home. Keeping agreements forces one to be pro-active, anticipatory. Megan knew there could be no excuses such as her friend's sister was late or the car broke down. She knew she was responsible for her own actions.

Hard-nosed? You bet. But tell me, if you've ever raised kids how many times *a day* do they break agreements?

Now you must be prepared to get back what you dish out. As you can imagine, at my house I better never break an agreement. Megan came to the office one day before the school year started and asked me to take her to Target to buy school supplies. "Yeah, sure," I said, my mind occupied by other matters. Can we make an agreement? she asked. "Sure." Look at me, please,

Dad. Are you listening? I gave her eye contact. I want to make an agreement, she said. When can you take me? "Thursday. I'll take you Thursday at four. Now get out of here, I'm busy." Dad, I'm hearing the words but I don't have the experience. Would you share with me your experience of this agreement. Sigh ... isn't true friendship the willingness to call each other on each other's crap? I look at Megan. "It is my understanding that I have made a commitment to take you to Target to get your school supplies on this Thursday at four o'clock." Guess where I was Thursday at four?

When we do break agreements, we tend to want to be reasonable about it. "The reason is. . . . " As you play more and more from cause, you will find yourself saying, "The reason I—oh, hell, never mind. I just blew it."

100 Percent Responsible

We are a nation of specialists. We each are a cog in the wheel, a dot on the corporate organization chart. In response, we segment our share of responsibility. If I'm a cog in the corporate wheel, then I cannot possibly be responsible for the whole wheel, let alone the whole machine. Let's see, there are 350 employees working with me, so I'm only 1/350th responsible. And if I can give my supervisors and the vice presidents and the CEO a little larger percentage . . .

But total personal responsibility does not work that way. Making agreements with other people does not in some way reduce your portion of responsibility for your experiences. Each party to an agreement remains *100 percent responsible for the agreement.* An example: You make a date to meet a friend, Pat, at 7:15 for a movie. You get eye contact with your friend, you both are conscious, you both agree to 7:15, not "Hey, how about a movie?" or "Catch you around 7:00 or 7:30." It is a definite agreement. Your friend does not show up. Just like Pat not to be on time, you say to yourself. Who is responsible for your experience of that agreement not being kept? Does Pat share some of the responsibility? Fifty percent? Sixty-forty? Ninety-ten? All of it?

Who is standing there in line craning his neck for his friend? Who has to sit through *Friday the Thirteenth Part 12* alone? Results do not lie. Of course, your friend is also 100 percent responsible for failing to keep the agreement. But you cannot sit there cursing your friend for your failure to ensure that your friend showed up.

What could you have done? Called Pat the day of the movie, or even shortly before you were to meet. Are we still on? Yes. Great, see you there. Your friend still does not show up. Who is responsible for your experience? Pat? But why are *you* choosing to make agreements with someone who does not keep his word? Does Pat understand the importance you place on keeping agreements?

How far does one go to ensure an agreement is not broken? As far as necessary. Communicate through modeling and through words to Pat that you have an urgency about commitments. Camp on Pat's doorstep if you have to, though at that point I would question the wisdom of making an agreement with Pat in the first place.

Marriage is one of the most sacred of all agreements. Yet marriages break up every day. Who is responsible for breaking the agreement? All his fault? Who had how much responsibility during the marriage? Fifty-fifty? Who had which half? Who decides who did which half? I did mine but you didn't do yours (this is what most divorced people claim). I contend that if you each took 50 percent, then neither one of you took responsibility for it at all. Each of you is 100 percent responsible for the agreement you made . . . and that does not add up to 200 percent.

While agreements cannot be divvied up, duties can. You can say it will be your job in this marriage to take out the garbage and it will be my job to do all the sewing. But if the garbage doesn't get taken out and the sewing doesn't get completed, who is responsible for the broken agreement? Each of you is 100 percent responsible.

You and Roy are supposed to produce an organizational budget for Susan. You and Roy make an agreement with Susan to have the budget on her desk in 30 days. Susan has gotten eye contact from both of you; she has gotten you to repeat to her satisfaction your understanding of the agreement to produce the report in 30 days.

Roy takes you aside after you leave Susan's office and suggests the two of you split the report up. You take administrative costs and floor space allocation and he'll take capital expenditures and employee benefits. You agree.

Thirty days later you and Roy are standing outside Susan's office. You have your portion of the report done; Roy does not. Susan calls you both on the carpet for failing to turn in a complete report on time. "Yeah, but Roy here didn't finish his portion!" you protest. Susan (who, of course, is also 100 percent responsible for experiencing this whole mess) points out that you both agreed to get the report in on time. You both agreed to be 100 percent accountable for that report. How you divvied it up was your business. But Susan did not make separate agreements with you. If she had agreed with you that you would do administrative costs and floor space allocation, and she had made a separate agreement with Roy for the remainder, that would be different. But the report was a mutual project. At that point it became your complete responsibility to make sure that Roy finished his portion of the project on time.

What could you have done? Checked with Roy every week to see where he was. If you were uncertain from the beginning that Roy was unlikely to finish his portion of the report (and you quickly learn in any work situation who you can depend upon and who you cannot) you could have made that clear to Susan and even gone so far as to refuse to make an agreement that included Roy. Or made it clear to Susan that she would have to put her supervisory pressure on Roy. That, or just figure you were going to have to do the whole report yourself. There were more options than merely "hoping" Roy would finish his report. Become pro-active. Become creative. Do what is necessary to ensure that any agreement you make you will be able to keep.

Keeping agreements is one of the most visible and most effective ways to model to the world around you that you mean business when you say you are playing the game called Life from cause, not effect.

Life is real! Life is earnest!
And the grave is not its goal.
  —Henry Wadsworth Longfellow

19

How to Be a Goalie

By now, I hope, in light of the fact you have read this far in the book, you have reached the point where you have decided you want to make more choices in your life rather than having them made for you. You want to take charge of your personal and professional life. You want to be more pro-active, productive, and creative. To do that, you must specifically identify some of the things in life you want to achieve or accomplish, what most people refer to as goals.

Unfortunately, goal-setting is typically an exercise in futility. Who among us hasn't come up with New Year's resolutions that didn't make it to the Super Bowl two weeks later? Benchmark birthdays are another great time to set goals. Hitting age 25, 30, 40, and 50 frequently bring reflection, a sinking feeling that life is passing one by without one quite getting a handle on it. These benchmarks spark a renewed determination to achieve some sort of unspecified happiness in the coming years, usually predicated on making more bucks.

In the business world, goal-setting typically takes the form of management by objective. That means management by the philosophy that it would be nice if it happens to work. A group of executives get together to decide what they want to accomplish over the next fiscal calendar. They establish an operating plan with specific goals. They do this by pulling out a copy of last year's operating plan and jacking up numbers for increasing productivity and reducing costs, and a catch-all called "improve the employee morale." A year later they get together to agree on the excuses they are going to use for not accomplishing the goals they set the previous year.

The reason they don't accomplish the goals they set is that their perception going into the goal-setting is that inflation, the economy, and turnover will be the external factors that will do it to them. They are playing the game from effect when they go into the process of decision-making. When one does traditional management by objective, many people hit an obstacle and say, "I guess we didn't want to accomplish that goal." Or they create an ad hoc committee to analyze it to death for six months. If, instead, they would start from an attitude of cause, of self-management, of being in charge, they would realize when they set the goals that whatever obstacles they experience along the way will be put there by them.

I also think many of us fail to even remotely achieve the goals we set for ourselves because we don't understand what a goal is in the first place. Here are some typical definitions I frequently hear. I'm sure you could add many to the list:

something you want to accomplish
an objective
a statement of future achievements
a risk
something to make you grow
an aspiration
a target
an ideal
a destination
a purpose

I offer the following definition:

A goal is an agreement with yourself!

None of this wishy-washy-if-I-get-around-to-it crap. A goal is a commitment you make with yourself. As with any agreement, you may alter that agreement if circumstances or your priorities dictate. You can acknowledge to yourself what you felt

224

at the time and what you feel now has changed. Unlike agreements with others, you are the only one who knows whether you have genuinely changed your goals or you are simply conning yourself. Are you altering the original agreement because circumstances have changed (despite your best efforts to be anticipatory), or are you backing out because of laziness or indifference or failure to be responsible for your own life? Like those New Year's resolutions, are you making *excuses* to yourself (often in the form of lies of omission)?

Let's test your goal-setting skills. Take several 8 1/2 x 11 sheets of paper. At the top of the first page write **5-YEAR GOALS.** Below that write out the goals you want to accomplish during the next five years in your *professional* life. Do you want to be making a certain amount of money at the end of the five years? Do you want to start your own business or change businesses? Do you want to change jobs or change careers? Do you want to become a supervisor or executive, or move higher up the corporate ladder, change departments, become a union official? Do you want to change the way you are working with your employees or your co-workers? Do you want to change your own work habits, become more productive, efficient, effective? Do you want to take charge of your own telephone, instead of the other way around? Do you want to work from cause instead of effect? Are there any goals you think will involve long-term change?

Once you have completed that, write out the *personal* goals you would like to accomplish in the next five years. Perhaps you want to start a family, move into a larger home, buy a new car, obtain an educational degree, travel to an exotic land, take up a new hobby or sport, spend more time with your family or with yourself. Are there personal traits about yourself you do not like that you want to change? You may want to work on taking charge of your life, be more open with others, less abusive, find less fault with others, be on time, be home more, make fewer excuses, relax more.

Now repeat the goal-setting on new pieces of paper for one-year, sixty days, and the next week. Once that is completed, read on.

Goals vs. Wishes

Goals are often confused with wishes. Wishes are dreams, something we'd love to have happen to us (notice the passive nature of that description). Typically they are not based in the now, but are imaginations of the future. Most of the time we don't take them too seriously, though they can be the precursors to genuine goals. I know a woman who dreams of being a cabaret singer, but who has no real intention of doing the things necessary to become one. Often the self-imposed limits of our mind prevent us from turning a wish into a goal. ("Oh, I could never *really* do that; it's just fun to dream about.) The person and the world usually are poorer for it.

So how do you determine whether you have a wish or a goal? I suggest the following criteria:

SPECIFIC
A goal needs to be specific. To say you want to be a better person is too vague. How do you want to be a better person? What specific behaviors about yourself do you want to improve? Procrastinate too much? Want to be more open with people? Want to remember people's names when you are introduced to them? Want to improve certain communication skills? Be as specific as you can make it. Setting goals means you must spend more time in your nows to accomplish the goals. Watching those reruns of The Monkees must stop (unless, of course, that is a goal you've set).

MEASURABLE
It must be measurable. You want to become the supervisor of your department. Very measurable since you either will or you won't. If reducing procrastination or living more in the now is your goal, it may be more difficult to put numbers to it, but if you monitor yourself you will know. Some people even set up charts. Each time you procrastinate or don't procrastinate, you mark on the chart in the appropriate space.

REASONABLE

It must be reasonable. Determining what is reasonable or "realistic" is one of the most difficult aspects of goal-setting, since people tend to swing wildly from one extreme (unreasonable) to the other (not ambitious enough). Perhaps, in the province of your mind, your sudden decision to enter a marathon this morning seems possible in that now, though up to this point you have never run more than one mile. Two miles into the race you recognize that the goal of the past now was unreasonable, based on your current experience (that is, intense pain). Note however, that you have run at least one mile more than you did before.

TRUTH

It must be the truth. Inside yourself you must have the intention to do it. That intention is what precedes all agreements Telling yourself that you're going to go to night school when in fact you know deep down inside that you have no intention of doing that is what I referred to earlier as a lie of omission.

DUE DATE

It must have a due date. Your goal is to buy a new home in two years. The due date must be reasonable. Saying you're going to earn a law degree in six months though you have yet to start your first class makes the goal suspect.

ABILITY

You must have the ability to achieve the goal. This is a yes or no proposition. A goal of competing in the 100-yard dash in the next Olympics is a wish if in fact you are permanently paralyzed from the waist down (though Special Olympics would be a reasonable option).

WILLING

You must be willing to do everything necessary to achieve the goal. This is often the kicker separating a goal from a wish. You must be willing to take 100 percent responsibility for achieving the goal. You must have the attitude of coming from cause, not effect. You must have the passion to take charge. Think back over the accomplishments of your life. Haven't they always been the ones in which you took charge, that you willingly took responsibility for?

If you can confidently say yes to all seven criteria, you have a goal. If you say no to any one of them, you have a wish. It is important to have a goal list and a wish list. A simple way to check which list an item falls into might be typified by something I experienced a while back. A couple of years ago I decided I was going to lose 80 pounds. Was it specific? Yes. Measurable? Certainly Reasonable? Yes. The truth? Yes. Due date? One year. Ability? Yes. Then came the kicker, the question you ultimately have to ask with total clarity. Was I willing to do everything necessary to achieve that goal? After considerable thought I said, hell no! I'm not going through all that crap to loose that weight. That sucker went onto my wish list. Later, however, I did reach the point where I had that willingness. I joined a health program and began to work out regularly, and I lost 35 pounds in the first three months.

Now re-examine the goals you listed earlier for the time periods of five-years, one-year, sixty days, and one week. Examine them against the criteria we just listed. Are you willing to take 100 percent responsibility to see they are accomplished? Are you willing to make an agreement with yourself? Put a star beside the ones you are willing to commit to. Now the goals have become a little tougher, haven't they? The lists are probably shorter. You may even find you have more wishes than goals. There is nothing wrong with wishes, as long as you recognize them as such. You are now more likely to keep the goals than before, since I think you recognize that an agreement with yourself is just as important as an agreement with another person. It requires the same effort to be home, the same determination, the same unwillingness to make excuses. It makes goals more difficult . . . and more achievable.

Goal Criteria

Stage I	Stage II	Stage III
Specific	Am I willing to	Ability
Measureable	do everything	Yes — No
Acceptable	necessary to	
Reasonable	achieve my	
Truth	goal?	

Date to be accomplished

_____

Goal Hurdles

In every moment of now we always do what we know how to do when we do it. That bit of tongue-tripping means our goals are based on our nows. We make decisions, anticipate, project for the future, plan based on the knowledge we have up to that moment. Ever notice how parenting expectations change from generation to generation? Our parents raised us differently than we raise our own children. They did what they knew when they did it. We cannot make them responsible for our nows. In the same way our goals of today may change tomorrow. "What one believes to be true either is true or becomes true within certain limits to be found experientially and experimentally." The ambitious marathoner changes the original goal after two miles into the race. But the new limit is simply a belief to be transcended by a readjusted goal. The runner will now set a goal of five miles, and when that is accomplished, ten miles, and so on until the runner reaches the original goal of a full marathon. Whatever the goals, you are the only one who has to be accountable to you when you change it.

Let's look at what possible hurdles stand in the way of your

229

achieving the goals you have set. Take a fresh piece of paper and answer the following questions.

1. List all the things you would like to have in your life right now but do not have.

2. List all the things you are going to have to do to achieve your goals.

3. List all the things other people do that prevent you from achieving your goals.

4. List all the goals you want to have completed and have not completed.

5. List all the things you would like to stop that are persisting and preventing you from achieving your goals.

6. List all the communications you wanted to get but have not given or gotten.

7. List all the things you would like to say to someone but you are too afraid or too embarrassed to say.

8. List all the things you are afraid to have people find out about you.

9. List all the people you are protecting, helping, and rescuing on a daily basis.

10. List all the people you do not think you can do without because you need them to make your life work.

11. List all the people who need you to make their life work.

12. List all the areas in your life that you are bitching about.

13. What if you took total responsibility for making your life work?

When my seminar participants do this exercise, most of them write furiously until about halfway through the list. Then their pens slow and they begin to look suspiciously at me, and finally expressions of realization cross their faces. Go back to question #1. You have nothing that you did not choose to have, and what you do not have now you chose not to have. Look at question #2. How about taking 100 percent responsibility? Put your shovel down. Or question #4. If you had wanted to complete those goals you would have completed them by now, but since you didn't, you haven't. Or #8. Why would you be afraid? We are all the same people; we are the same human beings with the same basic emotions, so there is no reason to be afraid. Or #10. Want, not need. Or #11. Nobody else needs you to make their life work.

You have no hurdles for your goals. Goals are agreements you have made with yourself, and you are the only person who can change that agreement or choose not to reach your goals.

There are no excuses . . . ever.

Afoot and lighthearted I take to the open road,
Healthy, free, the world before me,
The long brown path before me leading wherever I choose.
                                        —Walt Whitman

20

The Silver Hammer

I have had seminar participants who knew people who had taken my seminar perhaps two or three years before say to me, "They don't seem to be doing this crap, Ted. It's not working for them." First, it is nice of them to make that decision for the other person. Second, the person may be doing more than they realize. Third, it has taken each of us our lifetime to develop the attitudes and behaviors we have. To expect someone in a mere two or three years to radically alter their attitudes and behaviors is expecting a lot. Learning to accept and practice total responsibility for yourself, while not that difficult in principle, is tough to apply in a world full of people who believe they are being victimized daily.

My guess is, at this point you are feeling a bit bewildered, angered, confused, and uncertain about what you've read in these preceding pages. You have, like the Truth Seeker entering the ashram, passed between the lions of confusion and paradox to get to the truth. Learning almost always involves confusion and paradox. Remember learning to drive a stick shift? You look down at the floor the first time and there are three pedals and you've got only two feet. Total Responsibility Management is the same way. How can everybody be 100 percent responsible for their experiences? Doesn't that add up to 200 percent or 1,000 percent or 1,000,000,000,000,000 percent? How can giving what you want get what you want? Some of this personal responsibility business seems common sense, like locking your keys in the car, but that Bananaland stuff . . . And at times it's difficult to understand how you could possibly be responsible for some of the things you have experienced in your life. It had to be the other person's fault. Or just plain Bad Luck.

Putting aside for a moment all the confusion and the paradox you feel right now, let me ask you a question. Since beginning this book haven't you begun to notice one thing: how many excuses people produce every day? Don't those excuses leap out at you now? Even your own? Aren't you already less patient with excuses than you were before you started this book?

That's the first step to applying self-management to your life. As you grow more aware of how much we all play life from effect, and how paralyzing and depressing that approach is, you can then take the next step: to actively begin to play life from cause. You will realize how every now in your life provides choices.

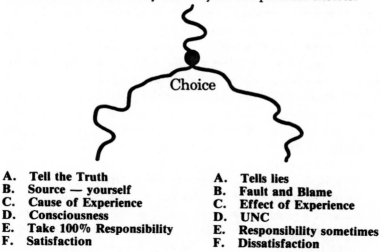

Choice

A. **Tell the Truth**	A. **Tells lies**
B. **Source — yourself**	B. **Fault and Blame**
C. **Cause of Experience**	C. **Effect of Experience**
D. **Consciousness**	D. **UNC**
E. **Take 100% Responsibility**	E. **Responsibility sometimes**
F. **Satisfaction**	F. **Dissatisfaction**

Relax

This is the tough part. I saw a friend recently who had taken my seminar a year before, and I asked him, "Dick, tell me which of the days of the program was the toughest. Was it the first day, when I threw all that new stuff at you?" Dick shook his head. "Was it the second day, when I talked about Bananaland?" Nope. "The third day, when I talked about the Circle of Responsibility and the difficulty of making it work in a world that doesn't care?" Dick continued to shake his head.

"No, Ted, the toughest day of the whole three-day program was the fourth day. That's when I had to do something with it."

My first suggestion towards doing something is to forget entirely about this book . . . at least for a few days. Put it aside and don't think about it, don't struggle with the concepts, don't work at applying them, don't even talk to anyone about it. Let the ideas and the principles and the examples percolate down through your brain cells. Let them simmer in your mind like your grandmother's chicken soup. If you find these ideas fresh and exciting, they'll stay with you. You may wish to re-read certain portions of the book later.

Another reason to let these principles simmer for a while is to avoid burnout. I mentioned before how most of us have attended a seminar or read a book where the speaker or writer captivated us and inspired us and left us pumped up, but that we lost it two days or two weeks later. We can't even remember the speaker's or author's name today, let alone what he or she said. What happened? Where did all that fire go? Part of the answer may lie in the practicability of the author's message. It sounded good, but applying it to "reality" proved frustrating. That's especially the case if the author was trying to tell you how to run everybody else's life.

More likely the problem was you simply tried too hard. One can only maintain such intensity for so long. The same with TRM. Since you determine your own "reality" that aspect should not be a problem. You will be frustrated only by the limits of your own mind. But trying too much too quickly can be defeating. The harder you struggle to make your life work the more it is a waste of time. If you try to turn your whole approach to living around in a matter of hours or days, you will burn out like a nova star. You'll fail like all those New Year's resolutions fail: born out of the heat of night passion, dead and forgotten in the hangover coolness of morning.

To make Total Responsibility Management work for you involves another one of those paradoxes: getting by letting go. In

India a certain type of monkey is a special delicacy. When the Indians want to catch it they take a coconut and cut off the top, clean out the insides, put a little bit of rice in the bottom, and tie it to a tree. Soon the monkey comes along, smells the rice, works his paw down inside the coconut, grabs the rice and pulls . . . and pulls . . . and pulls. That's how the Indians catch the monkey, kill it, and eat it. The monkey simply does not realize that to have both his freedom and the rice inside the coconut all he has to do is let go of it, relax, and turn the coconut upside down.

For TRM to work, you also must let go. You must get out of your own way. Remember learning how to ride a bicycle? Didn't you get the hang of it the day you finally let go, when you quit struggling like mad to balance that baby? Relax. Why do children have an easier time learning to ski or play tennis or do a hundred other things? Why do child psychologists say the child's mind from ages two to five learns faster and better than at any point the rest of our lives? Because they don't get in their own way. Their lives are not filled with all the hang-ups and boxes and self-imposed limits of mind we acquire by adulthood. If you are a golfer, have you ever noticed that you can drive every ball in the practice bucket 250 yards, but on the course you shank everything 110? I have a friend who, when he has a bad day golfing, quits keeping score, and invariably his game improves. We try too hard to make life work for us, when all we have to do is let go and let it work for us. Don't try—just do it.

You also do not have to accept everything in this book as dogma, as all or nothing, for it to be useful to you. In the introduction I likened this book to a supermarket. Take what you want and discard the rest. You know what's best for your life. You don't need to understand and accept the extreme situations, such as plane crashes or being responsible for being born blind, to gain something very valuable and practical from these concepts. Bananaland is there because I believe the logic of being 100 percent responsible for your experiences dictates that it be there. Accepting it is not crucial for getting on with ordinary living. Your life will improve immeasurably by applying these principles to your work, your personal relationships, and your day-to-day encounters with the world without thinking again about plane crashes.

Wrestle with the principles. Ask questions. Talk to your friends. Read other books. Get a second opinion. That at least is causing something to happen. Observe more closely life around you. Be home for it, and you will see, I think, how these ideas work in the "real" world.

I emphasized from the beginning that this book says nothing new. Most of us grew up with these concepts. We believe in them deep down inside, but have let a lot of other garbage get in the way. What I hope to accomplish is to help you structure those concepts in new ways, to add different perspectives, to make relationships where before perhaps you did not see them.

Newcomers to total responsibility living sometimes feel Total Responsibility Management should in some way *change* them. "Change" is a word bandied about in seminars, personal growth books, occult experiences, California hot tubs, and so on. Changing someone sounds as though the person is a robot and the guru is going to take out the "faulty" parts and plug in the "good" parts. I am asking people to alter the way they view things. I prefer to think of TRM as *transforming,* or altering, our perceptions. To transform something is to rearrange the basic ingredients: water into ice, for instance. I encourage you to transform, or rearrange the molecules of how you view the world and yourself. You are still the "perfect" you. You still retain your basic personality and probably your basic values. What TRM provides for you is a different perspective of the world, a different way to operate in the world. You will ask new questions, no longer content with the old tired answers.

Small Steps

People often tell me that though the concepts of total responsibility living are simple and commonsensical, they are not ready to apply them. As we have clearly seen, living from cause involves risk, especially in a world that not only does not understand cause but will fight to preserve its old and easier ways. Not all of us are risk-takers or are ready at this point in life to challenge those old ways.

I suggest you take risks by beginning with small steps. You probably have been "conditioned" for 20 or 30 or more years to play life from effect. You will not completely erase those habits overnight or in the next two weeks or in the next two years. Any book or guru who promises you instant and total change is a charlatan. Focus on one aspect of your life and begin to control that aspect from cause. Quit making excuses, and quit accepting them. Become pro-active. Develop and display a strong self-image. Be conscious. Be more creative. And notice the difference. You will notice a difference. It may be as simple as not letting service people give you the runaround, or refusing to buy into your employee's excuses. Whatever aspect of your life you choose, give more of yourself to the experience. You'll get more back. These small steps are the first steps to practical growth. You'll see how pro-active living really works, and you'll find it easier to take bigger risks, to lay down those artichoke leaves and expand the limits of your horizons.

The Rest of the World

As I cautioned before, total responsibility living is not a tent revival experience. If you believe strongly in these principles, don't rush out after reading this book and try to make it into a crusade. Don't act as though you've got it and nobody else does and aren't you the better person for it. Everyone is perfect or unique; you just happen to know that you are. If you attempt to convert the rest of the world by slapping Total Responsibility Living badges on the chests of everyone you meet, you'll find yourself alienated or attacked. The idea is not to preach total responsibility living . . . it is to *live* it. Don't attempt to drive that Circle of Responsibility backwards. Model it. Nothing impresses like action.

Avoid using the special language around those unfamiliar with *Unc* Fighter, choice, nows, scurvy elephants, Uranus, *chucas,* being home. Its use will only glaze over their eyes or offend them, and they will not understand it was their choice to be offended. Communicate what you do find valuable in this book in common language. Use "I" not "you." Level, don't dump. Take the responsibility to make sure they know where you are coming from.

During a break in one of my seminars, a guest at the hotel we were meeting in stopped me and asked me, "What the hell you doing in there?"

"It's a seminar on management development," I replied.

"What's it called?"

"The Management Experience."

"The Management Experience. You sure? I hear all this laughter, and people come out smiling and saying 'hi.' I never heard of a business seminar like that. What's going on?"

"It's a program on developing personal responsibility."

"Tell me the secret."

"Well, it's not a program with a secret. You have to come and experience the program."

"How long is it?"

"Three days."

"Oh, I don't have that much time. Just tell me the gist of it. Twenty-five words or less."

"I don't think so. It wouldn't mean anything to you."

"Hey, I've been around the block. I've been to more conferences and seminars than you can count with a calculator. Come on."

"Okay, I can sum up the program in two words."

"Great. What are they?"

"You are."

"I am what?"

The "We" Goal

Like many philosophies that focus on personal growth, total responsibility living risks being viewed—and abused—as a "me . . . me . . . me" approach to life. Indeed, many people and many philosophies do just that: stop at "I." But to me the purpose of all personal growth, the accumulation of all knowledge and skill development, should be to create a better "we." Most of us, I think, desire a better "we" in the family, on the job, in our schools and government, in the community, in society, in the world as a whole.

While each of us does not "need" other people to make us whole, the simple fact is most of us want to be with other people. From a practical standpoint, most of us do not want to return to that time in history where each person gathered their own food and made their own clothes and fought their own battles. We have become interdependent on each other. Cooperating with and enjoying our fellow human beings is a desirable goal about which few of us would quibble.

The quibbling comes in how we achieve that goal. Some would have us believe force of arms is the answer. Others believe the world would work right if everyone would just follow their particular brand of political, religious, economic, or social dogma—driving that Circle of Total Responsibility backwards.

As I've stressed throughout this book, for the world to operate in a way I think most of us want it to operate—more efficiently, more productively, with less friction, with more creativity and imagination and enjoyment—we must look first at ourselves. We must get our own acts together. People who do not know themselves, who cannot run their own lives, cannot work effectively with others. Look at any marriage that has fallen apart or any company department full of strife and inefficiency, and you will find at the root of it individuals who have lost control of themselves. In my opinion, the only way to an effective "we" is through a more effective understanding of "I." You are the center of your experience, and you and only you can control you. No one else can control you or be responsible for you, and you cannot control or be responsible for anyone else. But "I" is merely a starting point for getting to "we." If you stop at "I" you are being irresponsible.

Again, this may smack at first blush of narcissism, narrow-mindedness, egotism. It risks people saying to themselves, "Okay, since I am the center of my experience (hence the center of the universe) and I am the only one I have absolute control over, then I can step on anyone I want. I don't have to care about anyone else because I'm not responsible for them. I choose my own rules and play my own game."

That's anarchy, of course. With choices come complete responsibility for the results of those choices. (That's what the "me" generation missed.) The idea is to play the game called Life by the same rules. We may change those rules through mutual consent (agreements). If we do not want to play that particular game, we may work to change the rules we dislike or we may go play another game somewhere else. If you live in America, you have chosen to play by a certain set of rules. Democracy is one of those rules. In the rules of democracy you vote to have certain individuals make decisions for the rest of us. Whether your candidates or issues win or lose, you remain responsible for experiencing the results of those decisions. If that is not acceptable to you, persuade others to alter the rules of the game, elect new officials, or go play somewhere else.

Being totally responsible for yourself, and not being responsible for other's responsibilities, is not another definition of selfishness. Selfishness is the irresponsible looking out for one's self at the expense of others. Refusing to allow other people or outside events to control you is not a selfish act. In fact, if you do allow others to control you, you are allowing them to be selfish. Being responsible for yourself has nothing to do with gaining an advantage over others. It does not mean being uncaring, unconcerned, unwilling to help others. It is not a form of social Darwinism, in which only the strongest survive and to hell with the rest. It does not mean you are superior to others. Everyone is unique. Everyone is worthy of our love and respect, regardless of their behavior.

The "Real" World

So how does this concept apply in the "real" world? How does changing our own perceptions about how "I" approach my life make for a better "we" in a world rife with racism, poverty, AIDS, war and the threat of nuclear war, rape, political chaos, starvation, or any of a dozen other concerns?

Traditionally, these major issues have tended to focus on victimization, on making others responsible for what happens to someone. Individuals and societies look upon the issues from effect, not cause. Americans blame the Russians for the fact the world lives on the brink of nuclear disaster. Yet isn't it Americans, along with everyone else, who are experiencing the consequences of that reality, and thus are 100 percent responsible for that reality?

Five years ago nobody had heard of AIDS. People contracted AIDS before they even knew it existed, and thus could not take pro-active steps to prevent it. Yet, once it became part of their reality, they became responsible for it *and* for the results of their not being aware. Did they cause themselves to experience AIDS? Did they intend to have sex with that carrier or inject themselves with that needle or get a blood transfusion? (Yes, even babies who get a blood transfusion are responsible once it becomes part of their reality.) They also are responsible to the extent they allow it to affect their present nows.

We "blame" AIDS on homosexuals (though in fact, intravenous drug users, blood transfusion recipients, and heterosexuals also carry AIDS). Does that mean "we" have no responsibility for those who have contracted AIDS? No, the existence of AIDS is part of our experience, part of our environment. Indeed, it is conceded that AIDS in the United States will spread widely, to all segments of the population, by the year 2000. If there was ever an issue that the "I's" must take responsible steps (self-protection, abstinence, education) for the betterment of the "we's," AIDS is that issue. Yet so far we seem to be playing with AIDS from effect, devoting our energies trying to "fault" others.

Or take the issue of racism and discrimination. Most minorities and many whites have come to hold only whites responsible for discrimination. The minorities are merely victims. It sure as hell wasn't their "choice" to be discriminated against. Why would anyone want to choose that? Consequently, they are also in no way responsible for experiencing that discrimination. But their attitude only reinforces continuation of the situation. From my perspective of total personal responsibility each black, Hispanic, woman, or any other *individual* who suffers economic, social, cultural, educational, or political discrimination is 100 percent personally responsible for his or her experiences.

This takes us back to Bananaland, of course, since most people would argue that a person is not responsible for being born black or female or Hispanic. Regardless of your willingness to accept Bananaland, look at the situation of the person today. A black woman applies at a company and is refused a job because she is black and a woman. Is she responsible for experiencing that discrimination? Yes. Does that mean that those who discriminated against her are therefore not responsible for the act? Of course not. They are equally 100 percent personally responsible for their behaviors and actions. Responsibility comes full circle; we get back what we put out.

What is important, I think, is if you as a "victim" of discrimination recognize that "you are," in fact, responsible for your own experiences, then you begin to recognize that matters are in your own hands. People with such an attitude take actions that will help them achieve cultural, economic, political, and educational equality. Many blacks, for instance, have come to realize this. Who has done more to break down the barriers of racism than blacks themselves? Rosa Parks chose to sit in the front of the bus in Montgomery, Alabama, in 1955, a choice that sparked the civil rights movement of the 1960's. She was a woman deeply in tune with her own responsibilities. She knew the way to freedom for blacks was through blacks.

If you are not the black woman, and you are not the people in the company who directly discriminated against her, can we take the view that that's her choice, and consequently we have no responsibility? No. Any other person, such as a white male, is 100 percent responsible for experiencing the now of that black woman experiencing her discrimination. Once you become aware of that discrimination, it becomes part of your reality. If you believe the blacks are inferior and should be discriminated against, that's your choice and your belief system, and no one else can "make" you change. On the other hand, if you don't believe that blacks should be experiencing discrimination, you then have a responsibility to change your experience of that— that is, work to end discrimination and raise the consciousness of people to discrimination. You are not responsible for that individual black woman's responsibilities, for her experiences; but you are responsible for communicating the rules of the game more effectively, including helping the woman realize what she is doing to herself, that she has other choices despite her feelings of helplessness. Feeling guilty for someone else's experience and thus attempting to rescue the "victim" will only reinforce the situation, as it has in many welfare families.

The starving in Ethiopia are 100 percent responsible for their experiences, and the rest of us are 100 percent responsible for having their experiences be part of our experience. We are responsible for all experiences within our existence. If your values do not permit people dying of starvation on this planet, then through money and education we have a responsibility to help them learn what they are doing to themselves. It is important to give starving people fish, but while we're at it we need to teach them how to fish.

Take another sensitive subject: rape. Is a woman responsible for experiencing being raped? Yes. Does that excuse the rapist? No. He too is 100 percent responsible for his violent actions, and must be held accountable for his crime. Does saying a woman is responsible for her own rape experience the same thing as that old belief system, "she asked for it"? No. What it does say is that she made choices or decisions that led her to her experiencing that rape, even if they were choices or decisions she did not wish. More important, she is totally responsible to the extent that she allows that experience to control the rest of her life. Many women, so angered over rape, wife abuse, sexual harassment, and job discrimination, denounce men as unremittedly evil, who must be shunned, thus reinforcing the "victim" mentality.

But look at what has happened in recent years as the issue of rape has grown more public and women's rage against it more vocal. Many women, the ones focused on solutions instead of the problems, are taking more self-action to reduce their vulnerability to rape. They are taking self-defense classes, carrying Mace and whistles, avoiding situations more prone to rape, walking with dogs or in groups, being more careful who they date. They have become less willing to play the victim, less willing to accept it. They are making public protests, pushing for tougher rape laws, more willing to file criminal charges. They are, *by their own actions,* changing the climate that once accepted rape.

This does not mean that women cannot be assisted by men to reduce the frequency of rape; men (beyond the perpetrators) have complete responsibility for experiencing women's experiences of rape. It is part of a man's reality as well as the woman's. It does not mean that society has no role in reducing the climate that leads to rape, arresting and prosecuting rape offenders, providing counseling for women who have been raped. It does mean women must quit playing the role of victim. Women who recognize they are the center of their experiences, responsible for what happens to them, are women ready to take charge, women who are less likely to become victims.

Whether it is rape or discrimination or AIDS or hunger or nuclear war, each of us is 100 percent responsible for experiencing the existence of those problems, for their effects upon us, for their pollution of our societal environment, for the detriment to the "we." And only through the responsible, anticipatory, creative, pro-active, aware actions of the "I" can we create the better "we."

The Silver Hammer

Once upon a time there was a manager who ran a data processing center for a large corporation. The brain of the processing center was one of those new supercomputers that can do billions of calculations in seconds. The computer was humming along one day, cranking out reports and payrolls and graphs and spreadsheets and predictions and everything else a company thinks it needs these days to function well, when it quit.

For a moment the manager didn't do anything, he was so stunned. Finally he banged on it, kicked it, and cursed it, but it refused to run. Panicked, he ran to his desk and dug out a secret number he had been given, a phone number to the best computer repair person in the entire country. Hurriedly he called, and the repair person agreed to fly in immediately.

Later that afternoon a woman carrying an attache case and wearing a gray suit walked in. The manager explained what had happened and nervously asked the woman if she could fix it. "Let me look at it," she said. She went over to the computer, studied it for several minutes, and finally said, "Yes, I can." Great! the manager sighed in relief.

The woman opened her attache case, took out a small felt bag, laid it on the table, and took out a tiny silver hammer. She walked over to the computer, studied it a few moments more, then tapped it in three different places.

Suddenly the computer began to hum and began again to crank out the voluminous volumes of data. Ecstatic, the manager said to the repair person, "You saved my life! You saved my career!" After he had calmed down he asked the woman how much he owed her.

"Let's see, that will be $25,000.75"

The manager nearly choked. "How much?"

She repeated the figure: $25,000.75.

The manager choked again. "Would . . . would you mind itemizing that for us . . . for accounting. There might be a coupla questions . . . "

"I don't mind." The woman itemized it on a piece of paper and gave the paper to the manager who read it. The bill said:

Three taps of the hammer at 25 cents each: 75 cents

Knowing where to tap: $25,000

With the principles in this book you have been issued your own tiny silver hammer, with felt case. You know exactly where to tap in the game called Life. The decision to use or not use the hammer is your choice.

Glossary

Belief System Thoughts that we believe to be true. Often times these thoughts are communicated to us by influential individuals from our life. Example: you're clumsy, you're lazy, fat people are jolly, blondes have more fun, etc.

Blame The assignment of responsibility to any source outside ourselves.

Choice A conscious or unconscious decision. A conscious or unconscious action (choose, decide, author, act, do, create).

Chucas On Uranus, my planet, when you wish to feel guilty, you reach down and squeeze these little miniature guilt *chucas* that bite your ankle.

Conscious When an individual is both physically and mentally experiencing the same now.

Expectation The power to mentally visualize or think a picture that becomes the desire you wish to achieve.

Fault (see Blame)

Future A mental perception of unforeseen moments. Life is one big surprise party one day after another.

Guilt   A feeling of disappointment or anger about the result of some now—that now is over and it is much more productive to be responsible for that past moment than feel guilty for it.

Intention   The conscious or unconscious energy that precedes the process of deciding or choosing.

Leveling   The responsible communication of the truth—the sharing of my perception and the listening for understanding of another's perception. The purpose is win-win.

Now   The present moment—the only moment we have to produce results. Nows are experienced fully when the *mind* and the *body* are *together* in the same now, one after another.

Past   A mental perception of old nows.

Perception   Each of us has our perception of the world—that perception is based on *our* thoughts and *our* experiences exclusively. We only have *our* view of the world.

Perfection   This word does not mean ideal, it means unique. Each of us is tremendously unique and special, and we should view ourselves that way.

Piece   Our physical body; the form we occupy while we play the game called Life.

Responsibility That which is attributed to being the cause.

Risk   Growth is accomplished by challenging the way we have always done things. Accepting the fear that is associated with the unknown and viewing that moment as a challenge rather than a threat.

Time   All we have is now—the present—each of us has 24 hours in each given day. We have all the time there is—we simply are not home for most of it.

Unc   An abbreviation of the word unconscious. It's a much better word than daydreaming, but it means the same thing.

Unconscious   When our mind and body are in two different locations—physically in the present, mentally in the past or future.

Uranus   Another unique planet in our solar system.

Worry   Anxiety caused by perceptions of uneasiness or lack of control.

Worry Waves   On Uranus, the waving of our arms up and down to assure better control of the future.

Yamma Yamma   Mind chatter—the mind is always anticipating the next moment. Never being satisfied with the now we are presently experiencing, rather always anticipating the next moment.

Index

CPSIA information can be obtained
at www.ICGtesting.com
Printed in the USA
LVOW12*0706070317
526322LV00001B/2/P